Yesterday
as held
as shadow
following
Today
into Morrow

Credit goes to
the team of designers,
photographers, cartoonists,
and editor Dean Goodluck
at the publisher: D'Moon

Copyright ©D'Moon
first edition, 2021
all rights reserved
except for reader comments,
official US state seal images and
poems & quotes not by LuCxeed

ISBN: 978-1-933187-97-6

Slight variations may occur
as part of the print-on-demand process
since each book is manufactured in its entirety.

Your feedback is most welcome ~
publisher@worldculturepictorial.com

"There are three classes of men; lovers of wisdom, lovers of honor, and lovers of gain."
- Plato

"Look deep into nature, and then you will understand everything better."
- Albert Einstein

Introduction

Life haunted in more than one year.
So halted the publication of
Six Steps Wiser.
To greet light breaking darkness,
lifting up curtains at horizon,
folks step out of houses,
billions and billions,
pray for those fallen
"ashes to ashes, dust to dust",
thank the blessings for the spared,
wipe tears, be brave, carry on!

It takes courage to be as once we were...
Holding a book in hand,
reading is like a soothing breeze,
blowing away heavy
clouds cast by tragedy,
bringing back inspiration to aspire.
So here comes Six Steps Wiser,
to join billions, stepping out,
greeting light at dawn:
"hello blue sky,
hello blue ocean,
hello dear readers,
enjoy the fine-art quality book
of online-and-offline
learning and reflection".

When it comes to reading,
the leisure and pleasure
of holding a book in hand
is hardly replaced by electronics,
though computers and software
advance by generations.
Each entry in Six Steps Wiser
leads to an amazing story
(Zebra going to pub, 6.5mil trees planted,
$1.3mil vs $65.4mil/year),
character (Roger Federer), or technology's
surprising advancement (Hubble
Telescope, 1-wheeled electric motorcycle).
310 thousand readers love the story
"leopard nudges mouse,
mouse chews on".

Each of more than 100 selected entries
is a glimpse through an invisible window,
with a link for online exploration -
first underwater Cabinet meeting,
first Cabinet meeting at Mt. Everest,
first of its kind solar plane ,
first US library,
first lightning rod,
first shot of WWii,
first animated movie to open Cannes,
first US state,
first steel suspension bridge,
first adventure of Asterix and Obelix.

In print is also some readers' reflection,
a connection beyond the book,
beyond screen.
Gentle hearts moved,
touching comments jotted.
Millions of readers
have dropped by,
thousands have written messages
to share feelings and knowledge.
Readers' thoughtful comments
are truly inspiring,
and halfway testimonials
to bring these books to more people
as the famous do many other books.
Another uniqueness
of Six Steps Wiser
is to bring classic poems
into modern life (Section II).

Reading is pleasure,
reflection sows prudence
and courage for a better
tomorrow just as,
in one day,
volunteers
planted 541,176 trees.
One step forward, wiser.

Publisher's Note

Life is basking in fresh air, and science in Nature's law. The intimacy of Mankind and Earth may be forever as long as Earth won't be upset by human mindskills to alter natural layouts. "Inventions" are celebrated with eagerness. Imagination has no limitation, and capacity of Science? And can Science be invented ignoring Nature's Law? Sir Francis Bacon has his insight -

"III.
Human knowledge and human power meet in one; for where the cause is not known the effect cannot be produced. Nature to be commanded
must be obeyed; and that which in contemplation is as the cause is in operation as the rule.

V.
Towards the effecting of works, all
that man can do
is to put together or
put asunder natural bodies.
The rest is done by nature working within."

Year of Black Hole (2019) has caught a glimpse of universe's immmense energy and motion. To remake Nature's Law? The Interpretation Of Nature votes nay. Had that hinted to the clueless, Life'd be less stressed, Science, less streched. Sixth Step Wiser to a wonderful year ahead!

Dean Goodluck
Contents

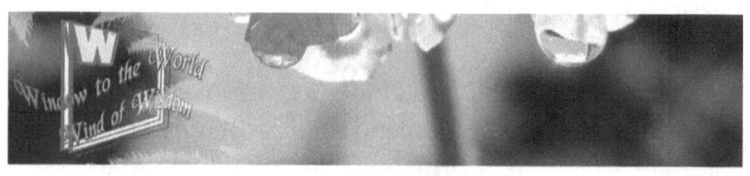

Beginning
Copyright
Title Page
Introduction
Publisher's Note
Table of Contents

Section 1

2009/05/01
"A Late Walk"
by Robert Frost
"I end not far from my going forth
By picking the faded blue
Of the last remaining aster flower
To carry again to you"

2009/05/02
Brazil impresses the world

Contents

2009/05/03
"The purpose of life
is a life of purpose."
- Robert Byrne

2009/05/05
Nobel laureate
reaches the age of 100

2009/05/06
Cinco de Mayo
6000 vs 2000

2009/05/07
Fun food: easy and spicy

2009/05/08
"Life is a series of collisions
with the future..."
- Jose Ortega y Gasset

Dean Goodluck
Contents

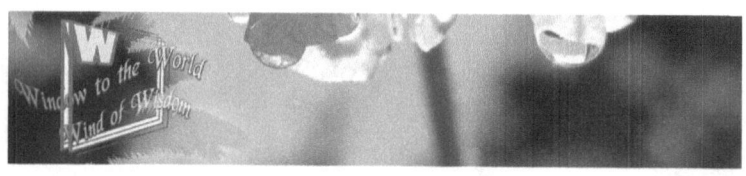

2009/05/11
One-wheeled
electric motorcycle

2009/05/12
"I arise in the morning
torn between a desire
to improve the world
and a desire to enjoy the world..."
- E. B. White

2009/05/14
Named after Edwin Hubble
pioneering astronomer

2009/05/15
"The human spirit needs places
where nature has not been
rearranged by the hand of man."
- Author Unknown

Six Steps Wiser - WeP Reading & Reflection Vol. 06

Contents

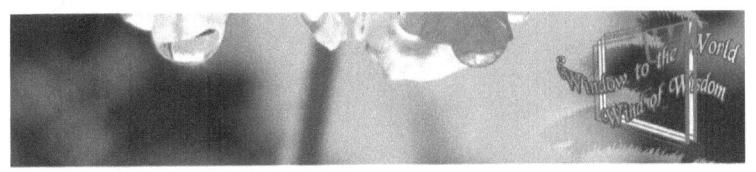

2009/05/17
Thousands of balloons
one dream

2009/05/19
Seaweeds, reflection

2009/05/20
Germany
Vauban's streets nearly car-free

2009/05/22
Australian beaches
1906

2009/05/24
"None are so old as those
who have outlived enthusiasm."
- Henry David Thoreau

Dean Goodluck
Contents

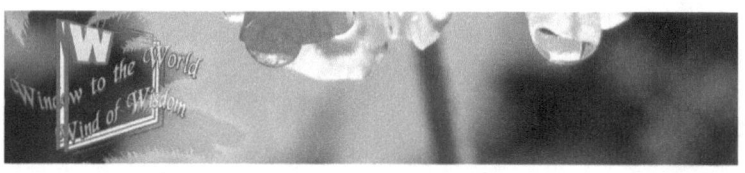

2009/05/25
1st Battalion
the Royal Welsh

2009/05/27
San Francisco
iconic GG Bridge: $1.3 million
street cleaning: $65.4 million a year

2009/05/29
"Life is a dream for the wise,
a game for the fool,
a comedy for the rich,
a tragedy for the poor."
- Sholom Aleichem

2009/05/31
Office Chair Racing

Six Steps Wiser - WeP Reading & Reflection Vol. 06

Contents

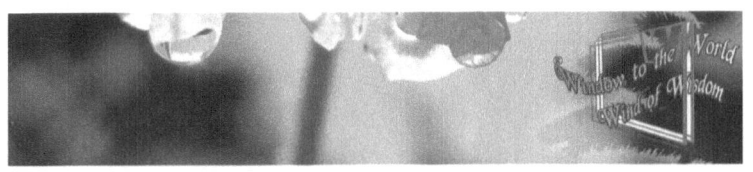

2009/06/02
Detective vs DNA

2009/06/04
Zebra
going to a pub

2009/06/06
Turning point
6 June 1944 D-Day
50 miles of Normandy beaches

2009/06/08
Pure speed
faster than sound

2009/06/10
Lightning rod
first library
first fire department

Dean Goodluck
Contents

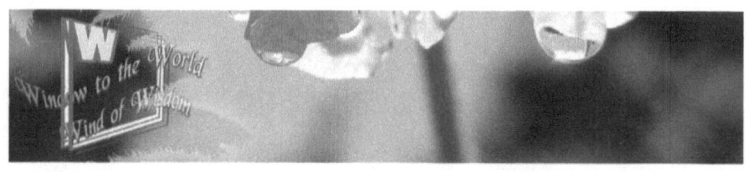

2009/06/12
Swine flu
Pig to Person
Person to Pig

2009/06/14
"Nothing can cure the soul
but the senses,
just as nothing can cure the senses
but the soul."
– Oscar Wilde

2009/06/16
Parks are Fortunes

2009/06/18
"It is said that the world is
in a state of bankruptcy..."
– Ralph Waldo Emerson

Contents

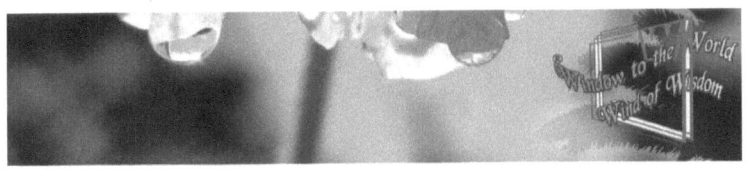

2009/06/20
Burma
Aung San Suu Kyi

2009/06/22
"The Gladness Of Nature"
by William Cullen Bryant

2009/06/23
Contrast
Nature's beauty
garbage trashed

2009/06/25
Fun with Nature

2009/06/27
This is IT:
Michael Jackson

Dean Goodluck

Contents

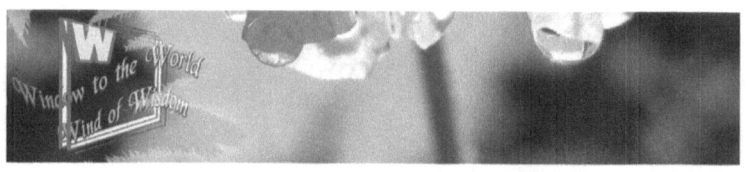

2009/06/29
Antarctica
679 whales killed

2009/07/01
Sea rising
city under water

2009/07/03
A good question
can you answer?

2009/07/05
Earth Song
by Michael Jackson

2009/07/07
Tennis
Roger Federer

Six Steps Wiser - WcP Reading & Reflection Vol. 06

Contents

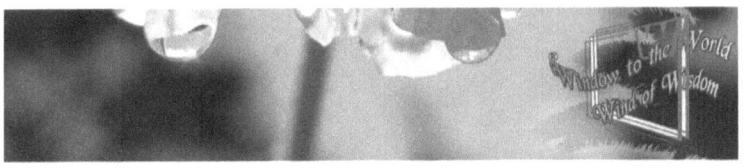

2009/07/09
Never a good war
or a bad peace

2009/07/11
Both
cancer survivors

2009/07/13
"O conscience, upright and
stainless, how bitter a sting
to thee is a little fault!"
- Dante Alighieri

2009/07/15
France
Bastille

Dean Goodluck

Contents

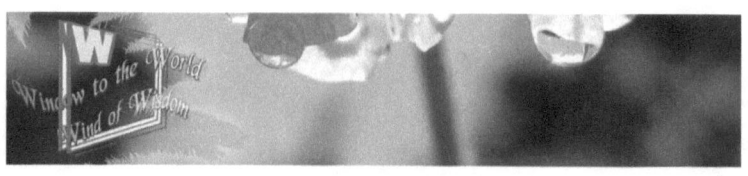

2009/07/17
Pakistan
300 volunteers
541,176 trees a day

2009/07/19
Remember him
Walter Cronkite

2009/07/21
Moon Trees
500 seeds

2009/07/23
Longest full solar eclipse

2009/07/25
Toddler navigates toy truck
12 kilometers downriver

Six Steps Wiser - WcP Reading & Reflection Vol. 06

Contents

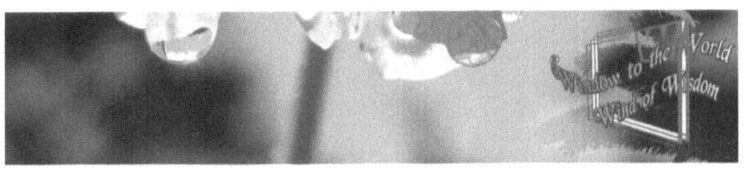

2009/07/27
"Age merely shows
what children we remain."
- Johann Wolfgang von Goethe

2009/07/29
Trillions of dollars
results?

2009/07/31
"Every mind must make its
choice between truth and repose.
It cannot have both."
- Ralph Waldo Emerson

2009/08/03
Movie
non-fiction book
Charlie Wilson's War

Dean Goodluck

Contents

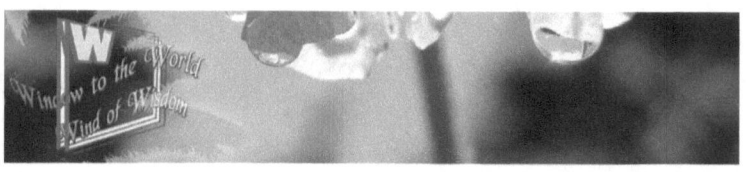

2009/08/05
"There is nothing more uncommon
than common sense."
- Baron d'Holbach

2009/08/07
Giraffes
join family breakfast

2009/08/09
London
8 August 1969
Beatles on Abbey Road

2009/08/11
"I don't know anything
about music. In my line
you don't have to."
- Elvis Presley

Six Steps Wiser - WcP Reading & Reflection Vol. 06

Contents

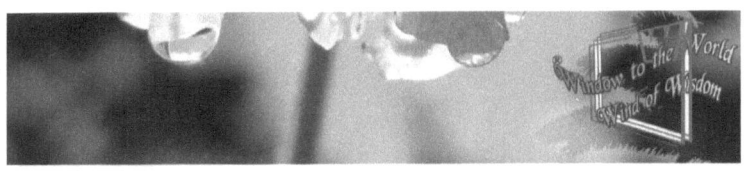

2009/08/12
Dr. Tommy Douglas'
idea

2009/08/14
Too large to handle
too expensive to feed -
everyone's nightmare

2009/08/16
Kenya in poverty
big spending
on trees

2009/08/18
Convenient cycling route
non-motorized trips

Dean Goodluck

Contents

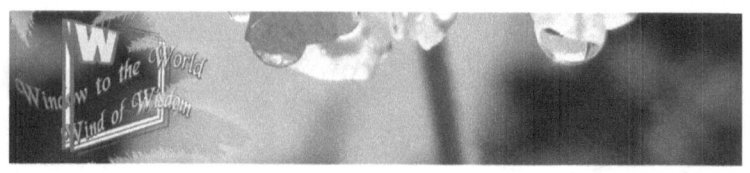

2009/08/19
"There are three classes of men;
lovers of wisdom, lovers of honor,
and lovers of gain."
- Plato

2009/08/20
Dolphins and
cultures

2009/08/22
"Look deep into nature,
and then you will understand
everything better."
- Albert Einstein

2009/08/24
From Iowa
to New York

Contents

2009/08/26
Lifestyle
can't be the same

2009/08/28
Heart beats
100k times per day
Heart disease
accounts for 1 in 3 deaths

2009/08/29
Measure
of a man's success

2009/08/30
Farewell
to all Kennedy brothers

Dean Goodluck

Contents

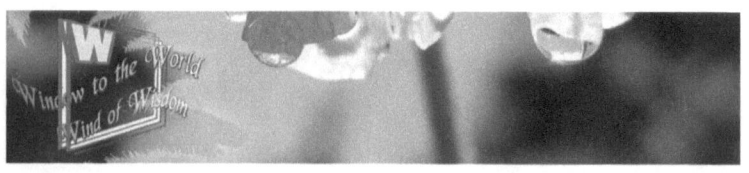

2009/09/01
"...not what we eat but what
we digest that makes us strong;
not what we gain but what
we save that makes us rich..."
- Sir Francis Bacon

2009/09/03
First shots of WWII
1-3 September 1939

2009/09/05
Skip the plastic
save a fish

2009/09/07
"There is no calamity greater
than lavish desires..."
- Lao Tzu

Six Steps Wiser - WeP Reading & Reflection Vol. 06

Contents

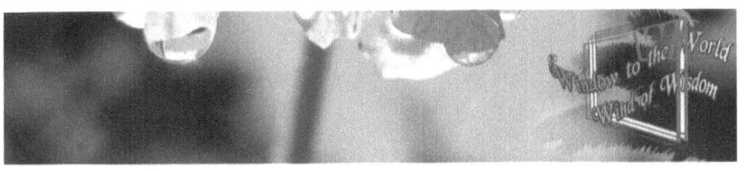

2009/09/08
Dolphin and surfer
who rescues whom?

2009/09/09
"We are guests to Earth
by chance /we own nothing
since birth till death
/but owing much to Earth"
- LuCxeed

2009/09/12
"Don't approach a goat
from the front,
a horse from the back
or a fool from any side."
- Proverb

Dean Goodluck
Contents

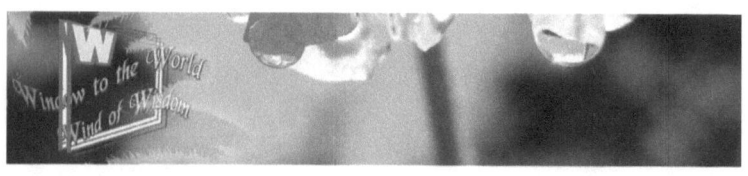

2009/09/13
"You are going to let the fear of poverty govern your life and your reward will be that you will eat, but you will not live."
- George Bernard Shaw

2009/09/15
Who did it?
Crop circles

2009/09/17
"We know what we are, but know not what we may be."
- William Shakespeare

2009/09/19
Fastest bike
by a total unknown

Six Steps Wiser - WcP Reading & Reflection Vol. 06

Contents

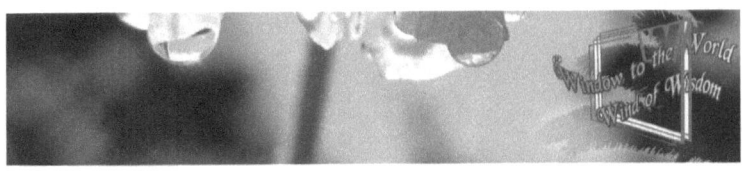

2009/09/21
"If we don't end war,
war will end us."
- Herbert George Wells

2009/09/23
Choice for mankind
sharing one planet

2009/09/25
"Without courage,
wisdom bears no fruit."
- Baltasar Gracian

2009/09/27
Verplanck Colvin
Forest Preserve (New York)

Dean Goodluck
Contents

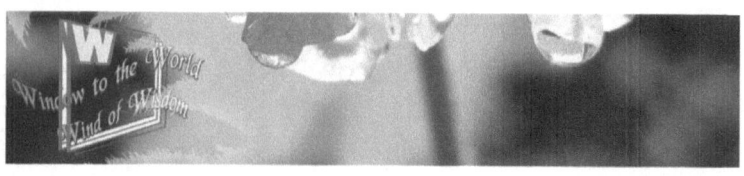

2009/09/29
Makeshift home
napping vendor
overloaded truck

2009/10/01
"Two things are infinite:
the universe and human stupidity;
and I'm not sure about the universe."
- Albert Einstein

2009/10/03
What inspires a kiss?

2009/10/05
"sharpness like knife
Shut in upon itself and do no harm
hand of Love, soft and warm
let us hear no sound of human strife"
- Elizabeth Barrett Browning

Contents

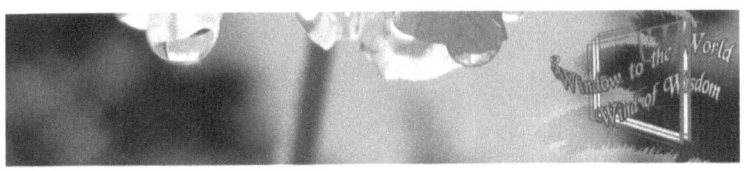

2009/10/07
"Spend wise - Guardian to Purse;
waste less - Angel to Earth."
- LuCxeed

2009/10/09
"We can easily forgive a child
who is afraid of the dark;
the real tragedy of life is when
men are afraid of the light."
- Plato

2009/10/11
488 hrs of footage
shocking aerial shots

2009/10/12
"Your living is determined not so much
by what life brings to you.."
- Khalil Gibran

Dean Goodluck
Contents

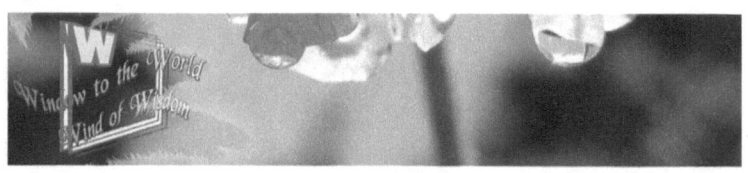

2009/10/14
Streets look different
on days without my cars!

2009/10/16
Q to Planet:
"What on Earth's the problem
with you?"

2009/10/18
Maldives
underwater
cabinet meeting

2009/10/20
"Things alter for the worse
spontaneously, if they be not
altered for the better designedly."
- Francis Bacon

Six Steps Wiser - WeP Reading & Reflection Vol. 06

Contents

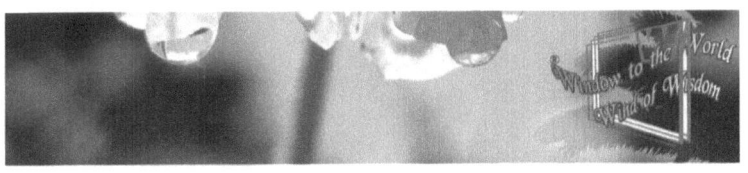

2009/10/22
Ice sheets melting
sea rising?

2009/10/25
John and Abigail Adams
marriage lasted 54 years

2009/10/26
"Good-Night"
by Percy Bysshe Shelley

2009/10/28
Solar-powered car races
epic 1864m (3000km)
Australia's harshest terrain

Dean Goodluck
Contents

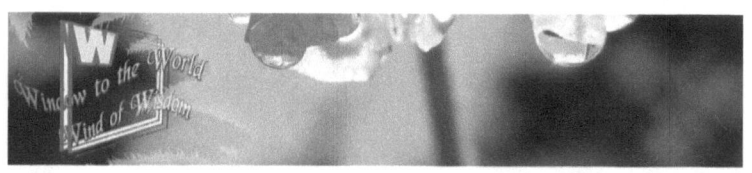

2009/10/30
Wily Gaul Asterix and
his clumsy friend Obelix

2009/11/01
"Moral excellence comes about
as a result of habit. We become
just by doing just acts...
brave by doing brave acts."
- Aristotle

2009/11/03
Mt. Kilimanjaro
85% of 1912's ice cap gone

2009/11/05
Who is
Lewis Gordon Pugh?

Six Steps Wiser - WcP Reading & Reflection Vol. 06

Contents

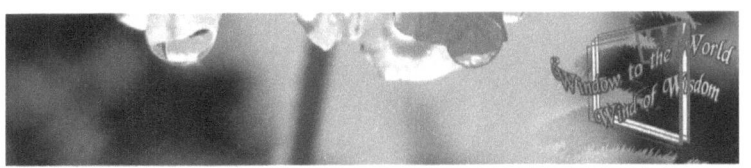

2009/11/07
Canada to withdraw troops
anyone left behind?

2009/11/08
8 Nov 1731
Benjamin Franklin opened
first US library

2009/11/09
"There's a smile of love/
there's a smile of deceit/
there's a smile of smiles/
in which these two smiles meet.."
William Blake

2009/11/11
Humor: shoe
size 7 vs size 14

Dean Goodluck

Contents

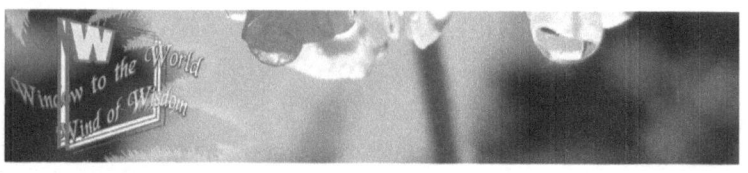

2009/11/12
"The worst pain a man can suffer:
to have insight into much
and power over nothing."
- Herodotus

2009/11/14
Spacecraft onto the Moon
to detect water-ice

2009/11/16
Veggie or meat
Your choice

2009/11/18
Gorbachev to withdraw from
counter-productive war

Contents

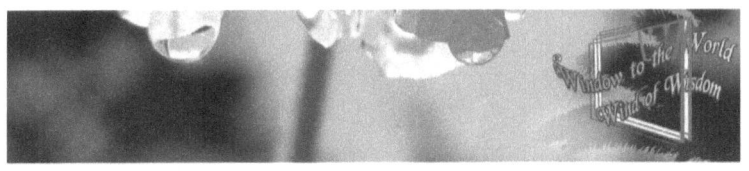

2009/11/20
"Humor is the affectionate
communication of insight."
- Leo Rosten

2009/11/22
Mouse keeps chewing
ignores leopard's nudge

2009/11/24
Annual loss
273 gigatons of water

2009/11/26
"Regret is insight
that comes a day too late."
- Northrop Frye

Dean Goodluck

Contents

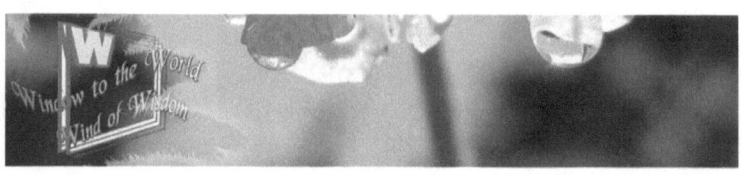

2009/11/28
Dubai catching up
debt, and
solar panels

2009/11/30
Spain, Italy, Germany, UK, France
ban "too-thin" Models

2009/12/02
"Nothing will benefit human health
and increase the chances for
survival of life on earth as much as
the evolution to a vegetarian diet."
- Albert Einstein

2009/12/03
Brooklyn Bridge
world 1st steel suspension bridge
opened in 1883

Six Steps Wiser - WcP Reading & Reflection Vol. 06

Contents

2009/12/04
Brilliant! Costa Rica
planted 6.5 million trees
$0 on military

2009/12/05
"Mountains are earth's
undecaying monuments."
- Nathaniel Hawthorne

2009/12/06
Nepal
Cabinet meeting at Mt. Everest

2009/12/07
7 Dec 1787
Delaware
first state of US

Dean Goodluck
Contents

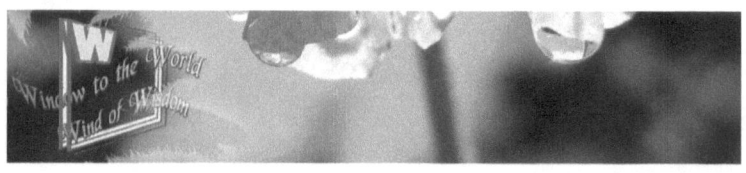

2009/12/09
Shared blue seas
free dumpster?

2009/12/11
Price to boom economy
sneezing and coughing in air

2009/12/12
Ocean guardians. Earthrace joins
Sea Shepherd fleet to save whales

2009/12/13
"A human being is a part of a
whole, called by us 'universe', a part
limited in time and space..."
- Albert Einstein

Six Steps Wiser - WcP Reading & Reflection Vol. 06

Contents

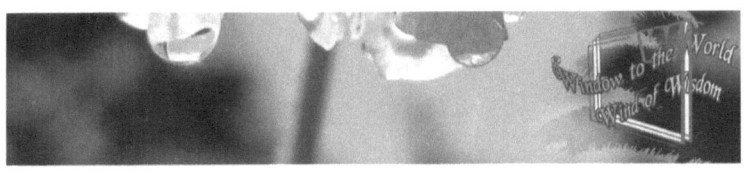

2009/12/15
Bargain with Nature or
remake Nature's law?

2009/12/18
7 Dec 1787
Third state of US

2009/12/19
"Ring out the old, ring in the new,
Ring, happy bells, across the snow:
The year is going, let him go;
Ring out the false, ring in the true."
- Alfred Lord Tennyson

2009/12/20
Snow fails no one
Ho ho ho, happy holidays!

Dean Goodluck
Contents

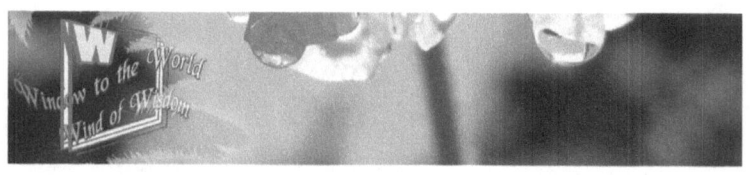

2009/12/22
Bertrand Piccard, pilot, aeronaut
André Borschberg, pilot, balloonist
Swiss plane: Solar Impulse

2009/12/24
ThinkAhead™ Calendar 2010
series to Health of Earth:
ice, forest and ocean.
Happy Holidays to all!

"In dwelling,
live close to the ground.
In thinking, keep to the simple."
- Lao Tzu

"Cogito ergo sum.
(I think, therefore I am.)"
- René Descartes

Six Steps Wiser - WeD Reading & Reflection Vol. 06

Contents

"Happiness is when what you think,
what you say, and what you do are
in harmony."
- Mahatma Gandhi

2009/12/26
"Robin Hood banker"

2009/12/28
Discovery Channel
"Whale Wars 2"
Most courageous volunteers

2009/12/30
Tonight
"Blue Moon"
2nd Full Moon within a month

Dean Goodluck

Contents

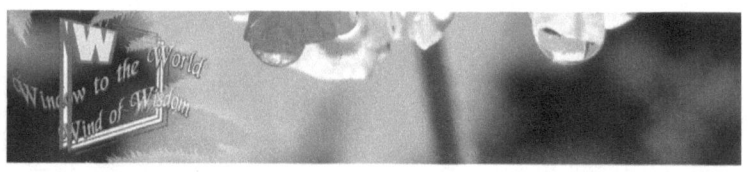

Section 2

Grape holds Wine,
Poetry Philosophy.
~ Leisure reading
along the Journey of
Publishing this Book

Poem
The Grand Consulation
- George Canning

Poem
Half-Waking
- William Allingham

Poem
In Memoriam (Easter, 1915)
- Edward Thomas

Six Steps Wiser - WcP Reading & Reflection Vol. 06

Contents

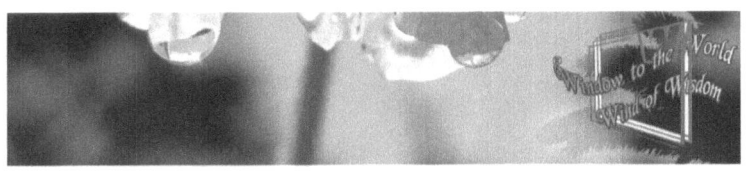

Poem
Paradise Lost: Book 02
(lines 1-154)
- John Milton

Poem
A Gleam Of Sunshine
- Henry Wadsworth Longfellow

Poem
A Farewell
- Alfred Lord Tennyson

❊ ❊ ❊

World Culture Pictorial®
WcP Blog
Book Covers of Other Volumes
in the Series

Dean Goodluck

2009/05/01
WCP.Poetic.Thought

"A Late Walk"
by Robert Frost

A Late Walk
poem by Robert Frost

When I go up through the mowing field,
The headless aftermath,
Smooth-laid like thatch with the heavy dew,
Half closes the garden path.

And when I come to the garden ground,
The whir of sober birds
Up from the tangle of withered weeds
Is sadder than any words

A tree beside the wall stands bare,
But a leaf that lingered brown,
Disturbed, I doubt not, by my thought,
Comes softly rattling down.

I end not far from my going forth
By picking the faded blue
Of the last remaining aster flower
To carry again to you.

Dean Goodluck

2009/05/02
WCP.WatchfulEye

Brazil impresses the world

2009:
Brazil leading in green power
50% of cars able to use 100% biofuel
70% of electricity from hydropower

2018:
3rd largest in renewable energy
2nd largest biofuel producer
500 wind farms in operation

www.worldculturepictorial.com/blog/archive/all/2009/05/02

Six Steps Wiser - WcP Reading & Reflection Vol. 06

2009/05/03
WcP.Life.Coach

The purpose of life is a life of purpose

"The purpose of life is a life of purpose."
- Robert Byrne

www.worldculturepictorial.com/blog/archive/all/2009/05/03

Dean Goodluck

2009/05/05
WCP.Story.Teller

Nobel laureate reaches the age of 100

Dedication and devotion - Italy's brain scientist and Nobel laureate Rita Levi-Montalcini wants to forget turning 100

www.worldculturepictorial.com/blog/archive/all/2009/05/05

2009/05/06
WcP.Story.Teller

Cinco de Mayo
6000 vs 2000

5 May 1862: Cinco de Mayo. French Emperor Napoleon III (nephew of Napoleon Bonaparte I, who lost Battle of Waterloo) declared war on Mexico, but was defeated by General Ignacio Zaragoza - 6000 well-trained French troops by 2000 poorly supplied local Mexicans

www.worldculturepictorial.com/blog/archive/all/2009/05/06

Dean Goodluck

2009/05/07
WcP.Observer

*Fun food
easy and spicy*

Preparing for a party, or fixing a quick dinner? Don't hesitate to go to tacos, quesadillas, burritos, enchiladas... Mexican food packed with colorful goodness such as beans, tomatoes, cheese, red peppers... healthy and spicy. Here are more than 100 simple recipes for any day of the year

www.worldculturepictorial.com/blog/archive/all/2009/05/07

Six Steps Wiser - WcP Reading & Reflection Vol. 06

2009/05/08
WcP.life.Coach

Life is a series of collisions with the future...

"Life is a series of collisions
with the future;
it is not the sum of what we have been,
but what we yearn to be."
- Jose Ortega y Gasset

www.worldculturepictorial.com/blog/archive/all/2009/05/08

Dean Goodluck

2009/05/11
WCP.Scientific.Mind

One-wheeled electric motorcycle

One of top 10 inventions of 2009. On the cover of Popular Science magazine is a 19-year-old MIT freshman. Ben Gulak, who first learned engineering from his grandfather, invented an electric motorcycle and won second place at the Intel International Science and Engineering Fair in New Mexico

www.worldculturepictorial.com/blog/archive/all/2009/05/11

Reader Comments

(not in chronological order)
- 2017/01/16 – "This is really great invention: a bike with single wheel, that is amazing and very interesting also. I want to appreciate this young student to get that kind of thought to build one wheeled bike and have safe ride on it. These pictures with the bike are looking wonderful still I believe that how can one ride on single wheel bike."

- 2017/01/16 - "Wow amazing."
- 2015/12/09 - "This thing is SICK! I'm not sure I want to find out the price tag of one though (estimates of $6k)... surely to be worse than the first model of segways."
- 2009/11/26 - "I like this scooter. Your article is is excellent. I love it very much. Hope to reading more content from you."
- 2017/10/29 - "Thank you. An excellent article."
- 2018/05/28 - "Informative post. You wrote like a children's book."
- 2017/09/12 - "Thanks for the information your article brings. I see the novelty of your writing, I will share it for everyone to read together. I look forward to reading many articles from you."
- 2012/04/26 - "I'm glad to read this information. It is very nice automotive innovation. Everyone should know that how & who the origin of this auto world. Thanks"
- 2017/09/08 - "Your article is is excellent. I love it very much. Hope to reading more content from you."
- 2018/02/01 - "Electric motorcycle is the common way of traveling through the different means in new occasions."

Dean Goodluck

2009/05/12
WcP.Humor

*I arise in the morning torn between
a desire to improve the world
and a desire to enjoy the world...*

"I arise in the morning torn
between a desire to improve the world
and a desire to enjoy the world.
This makes it hard to plan the day."
- E. B. White

www.worldculturepictorial.com/blog/archive/all/2009/05/12

Reader Comments

♦ 2019/10/24 - "This the best way to start your work in the morning. And morning is the time when we look fresh and it happens when we sleep at night early. I hope you continue this work."

Six Steps Wiser - WcP Reading & Reflection Vol. 06

2009/05/14
WcP.Scientific.Mind

*Named after
Edwin Hubble
pioneering astronomer*

Aboard the space shuttle Discovery rocketed to space on April 24, 1990, Hubble Space Telescope was undergoing final maintenance-and-repair mission before retiring in 2014. Hubble seemingly does not like the idea of retirement, so still remains operating in space in 2019

www.worldculturepictorial.com/blog/archive/all/2009/05/14

Dean Goodluck

2009/05/15
WCP.Philosophy

The human spirit needs places where nature has not been rearranged by the hand of man

"The human spirit needs places where nature has not been rearranged by the hand of man."
- Author Unknown

www.worldculturepictorial.com/blog/archive/all/2009/05/15

Six Steps Wiser - WcP Reading & Reflection Vol. 06

2009/05/17
WcP.Movie.Critic

Thousands of balloons one dream

A 78-year-old widower longed for adventure while some were conspiring to send him off to a nursing home. Where there's a will there's a way, and he found his way out. "Up" by Disney/Pixar is the first animated movie ever to open the Cannes Film Festival (2009)

www.worldculturepictorial.com/blog/archive/all/2009/05/17

Reader Comments

- 2018/11/08 – "It's a really wonderful movie I've seen ever. I watched it three times with my kids because they love this movie."
- 2010/08/25 – "A lot of good information, I come here all the time and am very happy with your updates, Thank you!"

Dean Goodluck

2009/05/19
WcP.Art

Seaweeds reflection

Le Vigeant, southern France: green reflections - photographer reflected in seaweeds at a plant which produces green fuel

www.worldculturepictorial.com/blog/archive/all/2009/05/19

Six Steps Wiser - WcP Reading & Reflection Vol. 06

2009/05/20
WcP.Tomorrows.History

Germany
Vauban's streets
nearly car-free

On outskirts of Freiburg, Germany - suburban pioneers give up their cars though car ownership is allowed. Parking space is available at the edge of the community

www.worldculturepictorial.com/blog/archive/all/2009/05/20

Dean Goodluck

2009/05/22
WCP.Observer

Australian beaches
1906

Sydney. Surf Lifesaving: voluntary lifeguard services and competitive surf sport originated in Australia in 1906

www.worldculturepictorial.com/blog/archive/all/2009/05/22

Reader Comments

- 2010/02/10 – "Great post and also information about surfing, really I like it, thanks for sharing it."
- 2017/05/12 – "I am sincerely glad that such events have become more frequent. Active beach rest is cool and best way to be healthy and happy. I have created a blog about this theme."

- 2017/11/22 - "WOW nice."
- 2017/11/22 - "Cool."
- 2017/11/24 - "Wow these pictures are looking awesome. I love surfing and I do every year in my summer vacation which I never fall at any cost. I even participated in many local and national surfing competitions and won many prizes too for my club and my school."
- 2018/07/12 - "Is it a good idea to send your kid to surfing school at the age if 11? If yes, can you recommend a good school?"

Dean Goodluck

2009/05/24
WCP.Life.Coach

None are so old as those who have outlived enthusiasm

"None are so old as those who have outlived enthusiasm."
- Henry David Thoreau

www.worldculturepictorial.com/blog/archive/all/2009/05/24

Six Steps Wiser - WcP Reading & Reflection Vol. 06

2009/05/25
WcP.Humor

1st Battalion the Royal Welsh

After eight years' service, leading every battalion parade - Lance Corporal William Windsor, Billy the Goat, retires as Royal Welsh Regiment mascot with full military honors

www.worldculturepictorial.com/blog/archive/all/2009/05/25

Reader Comments

♦ 2009/12/25 - "Very good post, thanks a lot."

Dean Goodluck

2009/05/27
WcP.Story.Teller

San Francisco
iconic Golden Gate Bridge: $1.3 million
street cleaning: $65.4 million a year

4,200ft (1.28km) long main suspension span, 8,980ft (2.7km) long, 90ft (27.4m) wide, 6 lanes, pedestrians and bicycles. 72 years ago today, Golden Gate Bridge finished construction ahead of schedule and $1.3 million under budget, opened in 1937, then both longest and tallest suspension bridge in the world

www.worldculturepictorial.com/blog/archive/all/2009/05/27

Reader Comments

♦ 2012/01/03 – "I agree that the Golden Gate Bridge is one of the most beautiful bridges in the world. I was always thinking to take a trip to San Francisco to visit the city and especially to see the bridge. I was always wondering if big bridges have staircases, from where you can admire the city and all the view."

- 2012/03/23 – "I just received for my birthday a 2000 pieces puzzle with the image of San Francisco. This bridge has a wonderful history and in my opinion is the icon of San Francisco city. The color of the bridge at sunset is absolutely stunning, like a fence standing against the blue sea. It simply takes your breath away."
- 2012/03/27 – "I was working for a Demolition Cleanup Services close to the gate and I gotta tell you, this is for sure one of the most beautiful construction that mankind has seen. The colors at dawn are beyond imagination."
- 2012/03/28 – "My favorite place is the park next to the bridge, it's an amazing view from there. I don't know if you know, but it is actually larger then the Central Park from New York. Imagine the quantity of yard debris removal coming from this area every month. It's impressive!"
- 2012/04/03 – "I am working for appliance recycling Houston and this picture stand in our office since I started working there. In addition to what is posted here I want to add that not everybody saw the value of building the Golden Gate Bridge and gaining the support took nearly four times as long as the actual construction of the bridge."

Dean Goodluck

2009/05/29
WCP.Philosophy

Life is a dream for the wise,
a game for the fool...

"Life is a dream for the wise,
a game for the fool,
a comedy for the rich,
a tragedy for the poor."
- Sholom Aleichem

www.worldculturepictorial.com/blog/archive/all/2009/05/29

2009/05/31
WcP.Humor

Office Chair Racing

Bad Koenig-Zell, Germany. Bringing office chairs out into sunshine, ready for a competition - 70 participants, helmets required, race on Odenwaelder street downhill over ramps... Many chairs didn't make it to the end

www.worldculturepictorial.com/blog/archive/all/2009/05/31

Reader Comments

- 2016/11/01 - "Wonderful article, informative and innovative. Keep sharing more articles like these. Thanks."

Dean Goodluck

2009/06/02
WcP.Story.Teller

Detective
vs
DNA

Even in DNA age we still believe in Sherlock Holmes, world's most celebrated detective created by Arthur Conan Doyle. Holmes phenomenon really took off in 1891 - the world celebrated the fictional detective for 122 years

www.worldculturepictorial.com/blog/archive/all/2009/06/02

Six Steps Wiser - WcP Reading & Reflection Vol. 06

2009/06/04
WcP.Story.Teller

Zebra
going to a pub

Bill Turner, a horse racing trainer who saddled 600 winners in 30 years, treats Zebedee (zebra, difficult to break in) with total kindness, winning over a friend from Nature, going together to the pub for a pint

www.worldculturepictorial.com/blog/archive/all/2009/06/04

Dean Goodluck

2009/06/06
WcP.Observer

Turning point
6 June 1944 D-Day
50 miles of Normandy beaches

Remembering history for future: 65th D-Day tribute to heroes who fought for world's justice and humanity's survival. The Allies of World War II launched the largest attack on German positions at Normandy on 6 June 1944 - more than 156,000 Allied troops stormed 50 miles of Normandy's fiercely defended beaches in northern France. Without D-day victory, the world would never see the turning point to end WWII

www.worldculturepictorial.com/blog/archive/all/2009/06/06

2009/06/08
WcP.Scientific.Mind

Pure speed
faster than sound

Photo: Ring of Water - F/A-18F Super Hornet hits speed of sound, water vapor in the air forms ring cloud around it

www.worldculturepictorial.com/blog/archive/all/2009/06/08

Dean Goodluck

2009/06/10
WCP.Story.Teller

lightning rod
1st library
1st fire department

"Do Well by Doing Good."
Benjamin Franklin honored what he said. His flying kite on June 10 1752 proved that lightning is electricity from charged clouds that can be brought to earth - he invented lightning rod for all of us. Also thanks to Franklin, for setting up first library, fire department, hospital...

www.worldculturepictorial.com/blog/archive/all/2009/06/10

- 2016/04/27 - "Hello. This article was really fascinating, particularly because I was searching for thoughts on this topic last Monday."
- 2010/08/19 - "Please give us more in the future. I will be anticipating similar entries with eager interest."

Six Steps Wiser - WcP Reading & Reflection Vol. 06

2009/06/12
WcP.Watchful.Eye

Swine flu
Pig to Person
Person to Pig

Pandemic swine flu spreads easily, cases reach 30,000, 18,000 in US; New Orleans mayor out of quarantine in China

www.worldculturepictorial.com/blog/archive/all/2009/06/12

Dean Goodluck

2009/06/14
WCP.Philosophy

Nothing can cure the soul but the senses, just as nothing can cure the senses but the soul

"Nothing can cure the soul but the senses, just as nothing can cure the senses but the soul."
- Oscar Wilde

www.worldculturepictorial.com/blog/archive/all/2009/06/14

Six Steps Wiser - WcP Reading & Reflection Vol. 06

2009/06/16
WcP.Common.Sense

Parks are Fortunes

280 California parks (listed) bring annual $4.3 billion to state, millions locally. 200-park closure to shoot deficit?

www.worldculturepictorial.com/blog/archive/all/2009/06/16

Reader Comments

♦ 2014/11/12 - "Hey I'm so delighted I found your blog by accident, nonetheless I'm here now and would just like to say cheers for an incredible post and all round enjoyable blog (I also love the theme/design), I don't have time to browse it all at the moment but have bookmarked it and also RSS feeds, so when I have time I'll be back to read a lot more, Please do keep up the awesome work."

Dean Goodluck

2009/06/18
WCP.Philosophy

It is said that the world is in a state of bankruptcy...

"It is said that the world is in
a state of bankruptcy,
that the world owes the world
more than the world can pay."
- Ralph Waldo Emerson

www.worldculturepictorial.com/blog/archive/all/2009/06/18

Six Steps Wiser - WcP Reading & Reflection Vol. 06

2009/06/20
WcP.Story.Teller

Burma
Aung San Suu Kyi

Burma's Prime Minister-elect, Aung San Suu Kyi, 15 years behind bars out of 21 years (1989 to 2010), turns 64 on June 19 (born June 19, 1945, Rangoon, daughter of Aung San, a national hero of independent Burma)

www.worldculturepictorial.com/ blog/ archive/ all/ 2009/ 06/ 20

Dean Goodluck

2009/06/22
WCP.Poetic.Thought

"The Gladness Of Nature"
by William Cullen Bryant

Is this a time to be cloudy and sad,
When our mother Nature laughs around;
When even the deep blue heavens
    look glad,
And gladness breathes from
    the blossoming ground?

There are notes of joy from
    the hang-bird and wren,
And the gossip of swallows through
    all the sky;
The ground-squirrel gaily chirps by his den,
And the wilding bee hums merrily by.

- from "The Gladness Of Nature"
poem by William Cullen Bryant

www.worldculturepictorial.com/blog/archive/all/2009/06/22

Six Steps Wiser - WcP Reading & Reflection Vol. 06

2009/06/23
WcP.System.Thinker

Contrast
Nature's beauty
garbage trashed

Staggering contrast. Untouched Nature's beauty vs human footprints: waste produced and garbage trashed: photos

www.worldculturepictorial.com/blog/archive/all/2009/06/23

Dean Goodluck

2009/06/25
WCP.Humor

Fun with Nature

Photos: plain cute - monkey's acrobatic fun; gazelle: "watch out!"; gorilla and girl whispering; baby deer's curiosity

www.worldculturepictorial.com/blog/archive/all/2009/06/25

Reader Comments

♦ 2017/03/30 - "I love wild life. World has full of beauty."

2009/06/27
WcP.Poetic.Thought

This is IT
Michael Jackson

Massive debt, stress, massive heart attack: Michael Jackson, King of Pop. This is IT: lasting legacy. Massive loss

www.worldculturepictorial.com/blog/archive/all/2009/06/27

Reader Comments

♦ 2011/09/08 – "Thanks for the great article. It was a fitting tribute to Michael Jackson. He was the biggest pop star in the history of music, and always will be. I have always been a fan of Michael Jackson and his death was a huge shock to me. If only people would overlook his bad publicity and focus on the genius of his music."

- 2012/02/10 - "I think many record labels wish they had been the ones to sign Michael Jackson, who was truly a legend despite all his personal problems and financial issues. His music stood out from the rest and in some ways bonded the world."
- 2012/03/09 - "Even after all this time, his music still lives on and his legacy to the world of music is still being counted. I think the strength of his music will undoubtedly leave him standing with the greats for many many decades and his rise to the top in popular music culture will be measured by his foray in music videos and the phenomenon it brought along with it."

Six Steps Wiser - WcP Reading & Reflection Vol. 06

2009/06/29
WcP.Watchful.Eye

Antarctica
679 whales killed

Of 679 whales killed in 2008-09 hunt in Antarctica, 304 were female. 4 lactating and 192 pregnant at time of death

www.worldculturepictorial.com/blog/archive/all/2009/06/29

Reader Comments

(not in chronological order)
- 2019/08/19 - "That's shocking how can a human be so cruel. I just searching some easy food recipe and then I found this."
- 2017/07/19 - "That's a terrible tragedy. I cannot imagine what could push people to do this. And don't tell me they needed money to survive, all the equipment for whales hunt is far from being cheap!"

- 2018/02/06 - "It's very sad news. This is one of the greatest threat to wildlife."
- 2014/09/25 - "Even if the government has restricted the fishing of whales, the hunting of the whales is still going on strongly. If the government doesn't take any necessary actions soon, whales would come under the category of extinct animals. Keep sharing."
- 2017/02/14 - "Indeed a sad state of affairs regardless thinking that 679 whales were killed in 2008-09 hunt in Antarctica alone, 304 of them female while 4 were lactating and 192 pregnant at time of death... tragic... is all I say."
- 2018/01/08 - "Very sad news. Over the centuries whales have been killed for a number of different reasons."
- 2017/03/01 - "Very sad news."
- 2019/06/18 - "Found your post interesting to read. I can't wait to see your post soon. Good luck for the upcoming update. This article is really very interesting and effective."
- 2018/06/25 - "I really enjoyed the page, well elaborated and well written. Congratulations on sharing the content with us."

Six Steps Wiser - WcP Reading & Reflection Vol. 06

- 2018/03/26 - "Thank you for sharing such a informative post with us, it will be beneficial for everyone. It is one of the best sites that I have visited. I am looking forward to read more blogs post from here."
- 2018/02/13 - "Nice post."
- 2016/03/04 - "I really liked the post. you are awesome."
- 2016/01/05 - "Thanks for making such a cool project. I've been checking the site but I never left a comment about it. I know you are working hard and doing it for free so you shouldn't feel rushed or anything. I hope you can continue this type of hard work to this site in future also. Because this blog is really very informative and it helps me lot."
- 2015/09/24 - "Thank you very much for the post. It was very interesting to read and to view the graphic images even though a big fish in general and a shark in particular is my biggest fear. I love this site due to its affordability and total customer-friendly policy."

Dean Goodluck

2009/07/01
WCP.System.Thinker

*Sea rising
city under water*

Earth has a fever? Rising sea temperature near worst-case prediction. Bear clings to cracking ice. Street under water

www.worldculturepictorial.com/blog/archive/all/2009/07/01

Six Steps Wiser - WcP Reading & Reflection Vol. 06

2009/07/03
WcP.Observer

A good question can you answer?

July 4's quest: which is more challenging for America, independence from Great Britain or from debt? Real time US National Debt Clock running scary fast

www.worldculturepictorial.com/blog/archive/all/2009/07/03

Dean Goodluck

2009/07/05
WcP.Art

Earth Song
by Michael Jackson

November 27 1995 released Earth Song written and composed by Michael Jackson: "...ever stop to notice / The crying Earth / the weeping shores? / ...we've drifted far". The song was a top five hit in Europe, and remains Jackson's best-selling single

www.worldculturepictorial.com/blog/archive/all/2009/07/05

Six Steps Wiser - WcP Reading & Reflection Vol. 06

2009/07/07
WcP.Story.Teller

Tennis
Roger Federer

World #1 tennis player Federer wins record 15th Grand Slam at Wimbledon: "There's no finish line. Far from done."

www.worldculturepictorial.com/blog/archive/all/2009/07/07

Dean Goodluck

2009/07/09
WcP.Observer

Never a good war or a bad peace

Benjamin Franklin: "There was never a good war or a bad peace." Children haunted by hunger, by horror, by poverty are all victims of War

www.worldculturepictorial.com/blog/archive/all/2009/07/09

Six Steps Wiser - WcP Reading & Reflection Vol. 06

2009/07/11
WcP.life.Coach

Both cancer survivors

Racing star in Tour de France '09 to win: Sebastien Joly thanks Lance Armstrong for support. Both cancer survivors

www.worldculturepictorial.com/blog/archive/all/2009/07/11

Reader Comments

◆ 2012/06/18 - "I love cycling and I never miss a competition when it's broadcast on tv. I recently bought myself a bike." I

Dean Goodluck

2009/07/13
WCP.Poetic.Thought

O conscience, upright and stainless, how bitter a sting to thee is a little fault!

"O conscience, upright and stainless, how bitter a sting to thee is a little fault!"
- Dante Alighieri

www.worldculturepictorial.com/blog/archive/all/2009/07/13

Six Steps Wiser - WcP Reading & Reflection Vol. 06

2009/07/15
WcP.Story.Teller

France
Bastille

Fête Nationale (14 July) is celebrated every year in France since the storming of the Bastille on July 14, 1789. The Bastille (built between 1370 and 1383) is four and a half stories tall, with eight closely spaced towers roughly 77.1 ft (23.5m) high. Bastille, once symbol of despotism, absolute power and terror, is now symbol of French Revolution and freedom

www.worldculturepictorial.com/ blog/ archive/ all/ 2009/ 07/ 15

Dean Goodluck

2009/07/17
WCP.Watchful.Eye

Pakistan
300 volunteers
541,176 trees a day

Bravo! Most creative, productive international competition to save the planet: Pakistan, 300 people planted 541,176 trees a day (the previous record held by India: 447,874 trees)

www.worldculturepictorial.com/blog/archive/all/2009/07/17

Six Steps Wiser - WcP Reading & Reflection Vol. 06

2009/07/19
WcP.Story.Teller

Remember him
Walter Cronkite

30 years ago, news anchorman Walter Cronkite (1916-2009) would finish up his hourly news broadcast to the nation of America by saying, "...and that's the way it is." Newsman, veteran, Walter Cronkite covered Allied Normandy landing in WWII, announced John F. Kennedy's assassination, and the Apollo astronauts lifting off for the moon

www.worldculturepictorial.com/ blog/ archive/ all/ 2009/ 07/ 19

Dean Goodluck

2009/07/21
WCP.Scientific.Mind

Moon Trees
500 seeds

Apollo 14 astronaut Stuart Roosa (the Command Module Pilot on the mission in 1971) took with him 500 tree seeds. The seeds orbited the Moon, but did not land on it. After Roosa's return to Earth, the original seeds were germinated by the US Forest Service and now Moon Trees grow in many places

www.worldculturepictorial.com/blog/archive/all/2009/07/21

Six Steps Wiser - WcP Reading & Reflection Vol. 06

2009/07/23
WcP.Observer

Longest full solar eclipse

It is Nature's play. Longest full solar eclipse of 21st century turns day to night in Asia - celestial show inspiring awe and fear in millions. Next longer eclipse will be in year 2132

www.worldculturepictorial.com/ blog/ archive/ all/ 2009/07/23

Dean Goodluck

2009/07/25
WCP.Story.Teller

Toddler navigates toy truck 12 kilometers downriver

Miracle: in diapers, with no lifejacket, toddler on 3rd birthday navigates toy truck for 2 hours and 12 kilometers downriver until rescued - the boy (in good shape except needing a diaper change) wanted to get back on his "boat"

www.worldculturepictorial.com/blog/archive/all/2009/07/25

Six Steps Wiser - WcP Reading & Reflection Vol. 06

2009/07/27
WcP.Poetic.Thought

*Age merely shows
what children we remain*

"Age merely shows
what children we remain."
- Johann Wolfgang von Goethe

www.worldculturepictorial.com/blog/archive/all/2009/07/27

Dean Goodluck

2009/07/29
WCP.Common.Sense

Trillions of dollars results?

2009: US could provide Medicare for all citizens as Canada does if some war spending ($891,971,525,495 since 2001) spared
2019: Brown University study, spending in Iraq and Afghanistan - $6.4 trillion (2001-2020)

www.worldculturepictorial.com/blog/archive/all/2009/07/29

2009/07/31
WcP.Philosophy

Every mind must make its choice between truth and repose. It cannot have both

"Every mind must make its choice between truth and repose. It cannot have both."
- Ralph Waldo Emerson

www.worldculturepictorial.com/blog/archive/all/2009/07/31

Dean Goodluck

2009/08/02
WCP.Movie.Critic

Movie
non-fiction book
Charlie Wilson's War

Charm of Diplomacy. Remembers trio who ended Afghan war: Joanne Herring, Charlie Wilson, Avrakotos ("Charlie Wilson's War")

www.worldculturepictorial.com/blog/archive/all/2009/08/02

Reader Comments

- 2016/09/14 – "I have watched this movie, which was directed very well and all the actors play a good role in this movie. After watching this film, I became a fan of the director who's really done a fantastic job."
- 2010/03/17 – "Great Article! Thanks for posting it."

Six Steps Wiser - WCP Reading & Reflection Vol. 06

2009/08/05
WCP.Common.Sense

There is nothing more uncommon than common sense

"There is nothing more uncommon than common sense."
- Baron d'Holbach (Good Sense, 1753), cited by Thomas Chalmers (Natural Theology, 1836)

www.worldculturepictorial.com/blog/archive/all/2009/08/05

Reader Comments

- 2009/11/18 - "Or, perhaps, someone much earlier: WHEN we coolly examine the opinions of men, we are surprised to find, that even in those opinion, which they regard as the most essential, nothing is more uncommon than common sense"
- 2011/11/29 - "Thomas Chalmers 1836, Natural Theology, Bk. II, Ch. III : On the Strength of the Evidences for a God in the Phenomena of Visible and External Nature"

Dean Goodluck

2009/08/07
WCP.Humor

Giraffes join family breakfast

World's tallest animal: Rarest endangered Rothschild giraffes join family breakfast; unlikely bond with short goat at first sight

www.worldculturepictorial.com/blog/archive/all/2009/08/07

Reader Comments

(not in chronological order)
- 2017/07/28 – "This is truly amazing! A strong proof that men and animals can become best friends, regardless the size. Although owning a giraffe must be quite exciting, most people prefer a dog or a cat, as pets. Some shelter dogs might be injured, but nothing that a leg brace can't heal in a few days. If you want a dog or a cat, adopt one from a shelter, they too deserve to be loved!"

- 2012/05/25 - "Guys I love giraffes. And how adorable is this little fellow? I think they are one of the most adorable creatures in the world. I am interested in finding any shops with books about them. If someone knows something please let me know. Thanks for the heads-up."
- 2012/08/05 - "Hey Andrew, you should check out this book - Jaspa's Journey: The Great Migration by Rich Meyrick. It's an adventure novel about Jaspa, a little giraffe - only 8cm tall. He's actually a distant relative of a Giraffe known as a Giraffeses. It's a fantastic book! It recently became available as an ebook at Smashwords."
- 2016/01/05 - "I'm really surprised to see this pictures. The giraffe is sharing a breakfast with the kid and the friendship with the goat. I must say everyone must learn from this animal, which was perfect in its steps and relations with others."
- 2015/05/09 - "These are awesome pictures of giraffes."
- 2012/01/05 - "This story is so interesting and the Giraffe is just amazing. From these pictures you can say how sweet and friendly Gerald the giraffe is with Eddie the goat. Last week when I was into the pet shop to buy on of those dog tags for dogs I was surprised to see a new pet there - a tiny creature that has been gaining popularity as a pet all across the country, the sugar glider. I love

Dean Goodluck

2009/08/09
WcP.Art

London
8 August 1969
Beatles on Abbey Road

Tribute to Abbey Road (40 years ago, 08/08/69), to Beatles: John Lennon, Paul McCartney, George Harrison and Ringo Starr. Brian Southall: "A policeman held up the traffic, the band walked back and forth a few times and that was that"

www.worldculturepictorial.com/blog/archive/all/2009/08/09

Six Steps Wiser - WcP Reading & Reflection Vol. 06

2009/08/11
WcP.Art

I don't know
anything about music.
In my line you don't have to

"I don't know anything about music.
In my line you don't have to."
- Elvis Presley, King of Rock 'n' Roll

www.worldculturepictorial.com/blog/archive/all/2009/08/11

Dean Goodluck

2009/08/12
WCP.Story.Teller

Dr. Tommy Douglas' idea

Tommy Douglas, Canada's father of Medicare, would import foreign doctors to make his plan work.
"My friends, watch out for the little fellow with an idea." - Tommy Douglas, 1961

www.worldculturepictorial.com/blog/archive/all/2009/08/12

Six Steps Wiser - WcP Reading & Reflection Vol. 06

2009/08/14
WcP.Observer

Too large to handle too expensive to feed - everyone's nightmare

Invited harm. 150,000 pythons out of control, spreading... near daycare, hospital; toddler strangled: a 17-feet-long 26-inches-in-diameter Burmese python was caught on a Hospital's grounds

www.worldculturepictorial.com/blog/archive/all/2009/08/14

Reader Comments

- 2012/01/29 - "This is really scary to know... I'd like to wish all the best to all the authorities who're trying hard to keep people safe from these deadly pythons."
- 2016/05/07 - "I think that labeling the pythons as deadly is inaccurate, at least to humans, these big snakes may be deadly but to the native wildlife."
- 2016/05/16 - "This is exactly right, these aren't deadly snakes on the hunt for humans, but they may wreak havoc among the native wildlife."

Dean Goodluck

2009/08/16
WCP.System.Thinker

Kenya in poverty big spending on trees

Kenya in poverty ($857 GDP/capita, world ranking 146) pledges to spend $20 billion and plant 7.6 billion trees. Imagine wealthy nations spending big on tree planting as well?
Top 24 rich countries' GDP ranges from $39,306 to $114,234

www.worldculturepictorial.com/blog/archive/all/2009/08/16

Reader Comments

- 2009/08/16 - *"Very informative post. There are many other nations with depleting forests. We just hope that in each of those nations, their government would look into this issue and would help fight for forest depletion."*
- 2014/10/09 - *"Great post. I'm really impressed by your site. You've performed an excellent job. I will suggest to my friends. I'm sure they'll be benefited from this web site."*

Six Steps Wiser - WcP Reading & Reflection Vol. 06

2009/08/18
WcP.System.Thinker

Convenient cycling route non-motorized trips

In fashion: cycling maps, bike routes
bicycle tours in Europe
connecting America by bicycle: 14,000 miles in 27 states

www.worldculturepictorial.com/blog/archive/all/2009/08/18

Reader Comments

- 2017/07/31 – "However, you might think that those routes are only for people that are very fit and in a terrific shape. Which is not true because they are not made in a way to be only a sports activity. You choose you rhythm, stages. And most importantly, EuroVelo doesn't have a goal to build tracks for cyclists but for people who cycle."

Dean Goodluck

2009/08/19
WCP.Poetic.Thought

There are three classes of men;
lovers of wisdom, lovers of honor,
and lovers of gain

"There are three classes of men;
lovers of wisdom
lovers of honor,
and lovers of gain."
- Plato

www.worldculturepictorial.com/blog/archive/all/2009/08/19

2009/08/20
WcP.Movie.Critic

Dolphins and cultures

23,000 dolphins slaughtered each year in hidden COVE in Japan. In US? $1500-3500 reward to get the one who killed a dolphin

www.worldculturepictorial.com/blog/archive/all/2009/08/20

Reader Comments

♦ 2016/04/08 - "I read your article you shared, are more articles like this having good knowledge."

Dean Goodluck

2009/08/22
WCP.Philosophy

Look deep into nature, and then you will understand everything better

"Look deep into nature, and then you will understand everything better."
- Albert Einstein

www.worldculturepictorial.com/blog/archive/all/2009/08/22

Six Steps Wiser - WcP Reading & Reflection Vol. 06

2009/08/24
WcP.Story.Teller

From Iowa to New York

Actor Ashton Kutcher reveals what's missing in drama business: hometown, genuine quality; and his "daunting" experience in NYC

www.worldculturepictorial.com/ blog/ archive/ all/ 2009/ 08/ 24

Dean Goodluck

2009/08/26
WCP.Life.Coach

Lifestyle can't be the same

Kids jumping high in nature in photo vs manmade crowed city Tokyo with population 12,369,000 (density 5,655/sq km)

www.worldculturepictorial.com/blog/archive/all/2009/08/26

Reader Comments

- 2018/03/01 - "Nice. Good quality post and comments, thanks everyone. I read good idea. I like it. Thank you for sharing blog post with us."
- 2018/01/17 - "It's really a one of a kind journey and it's really for a good cause. I'll admit I was never really that much into pro-ecological organizations, but the way those guys show their point, I'd support it any time."

- 2016/06/16 - "Those are great photos. But I like kids jumping high in nature photo because its awesome. Looking at the kids jump in nature makes me happy not like the other one."
- 2015/10/06 - "As human beings it is our duty to save the data of the past and present for the future in any other formats. Either in written, pictures, paintings etc. One can save the present conditions going around him. This way we can save the world culture."

Dean Goodluck

2009/08/28
WCP.Life.Coach

Heart beats 100k times per day
Heart disease accounts for 1 in 3 deaths

As English Proverb goes: "Don't dig your grave with your own knife and fork." Eat less meat, prevent blockage: heart beats 100k times/day, pumps 3-5k gallons of blood through 60k miles of vessels. Health and diet: we are what we eat. Probably true

www.worldculturepictorial.com/blog/archive/all/2009/08/28

Reader Comments

♦ 2009/09/04 - "Love the images on this blog..there are some interesting articles about health I noticed...we tend to run a 50/50 risk of a heart attack...I noticed when in the USA recently everyone seemed huge..they ate massive meals...I reckon that is one cause of heart failure...just my opinion..but yeah these articles can be worrying to some folk so just heed the advice...I know I will."

Six Steps Wiser - WcP Reading & Reflection Vol. 06

2009/08/29
WcP.Story.Teller

Measure of a man's success

"The measure of a man's success in life is not the money he's made. It's the kind of family he has raised." - Joseph Kennedy Bobby described his father, "We were to try harder than anyone else, we might not be the best, and none of us were, but we were to make the effort to be the best."

www.worldculturepictorial.com/blog/archive/all/2009/08/29

Dean Goodluck

2009/08/30
WCP.Story.Teller

Farewell to all Kennedy brothers

Edward Moore Kennedy (born on Feb 22, 1932) died on August 25 2009 and was buried near his brothers John and Robert at Arlington National Cemetery. "Thank you, Teddy (Edward Kennedy), for fighting for my civil rights." Farewell to all Kennedy brothers, all with courage!

www.worldculturepictorial.com/blog/archive/all/2009/08/30

Reader Comments

♦ 2010/02/27 – "I can't say this about very many people, but I have and will always want to grow up to be JUST LIKE JFK, TED, & BOBBY, what great men they were. as a youngster they are a great inspiration to me."

- 2009/09/03 - "He will indeed be missed. He is a great political icon and has fought for what is right and just for the people of America. There is none like him and I hope that in the right time, his dreams for our country will come true."

Dean Goodluck

2009/09/01
WCP.Philosophy

...not what we eat but what we digest that makes us strong...

"It's not what we eat but what we digest
that makes us strong;
not what we gain but what we save
that makes us rich;
not what we read but what we remember
that makes us learned;
and not what we profess
but what we practice
that gives us integrity."
- Sir Francis Bacon

www.worldculturepictorial.com/blog/archive/all/2009/09/01

Six Steps Wiser - WcP Reading & Reflection Vol. 06

2009/09/03
WcP.Observer

First shots of WWII
1-3 September 1939

The German invasion of Poland began on 1 September 1939 - at 4:45am on 1 Sept, the German battleship Schleswig-Holstein on a "friendly visit" to Danzig (semi-autonomous city-state, existed between 1920 and 1939).
3 Sept 1939, torpedo fired by a German U-boat sank British passenger ship SS Athenia.
France and Britain had pacts with Poland and declared war on Germany on 3 September 1939

www.worldculturepictorial.com/blog/archive/all/2009/09/03

Dean Goodluck

2009/09/05
WCP.WatchfulEye

*Skip the plastic
save a fish*

Texas-sized ocean garbage vortex found in Pacific. Bottlecaps, bags and wrappers end up in the ocean drifting thousands of miles. Plastic sea trash doesn't biodegrade

www.worldculturepictorial.com/blog/archive/all/2009/09/05

Reader Comments

♦ 2016/03/03 - "Unfortunately, the number of marine mammals' trash-related deaths are increasing each year. Our actions are to blame, but can we undo this? For many people, fishing is a sport, the commercial fishing boats for sale rates stand as proof, but for some people, fishing means subsistence, so we must do something to protect marine life, for as much as we can."

Six Steps Wiser - WcP Reading & Reflection Vol. 06

2009/09/07
WcP.Philosophy

There is no calamity greater than lavish desires...

"There is no calamity greater
than lavish desires.
There is no greater guilt than discontentment.
And there is not greater disaster than greed."
- Lao Tzu

www.worldculturepictorial.com/blog/archive/all/2009/09/07

Dean Goodluck

2009/09/08
WCP.Story.Teller

Dolphin and surfer who rescues whom?

True stories: dolphin answers whales' SOS call; pod of dolphins save severely-injured surfer from becoming shark bait

www.worldculturepictorial.com/blog/archive/all/2009/09/08

Reader Comments

- 2009/09/26 – "The arguments of the proponents of the continued mistreatment or slaughter of whales and dolphins are akin to saying that because humans are not endangered, and because we have been killing each other for millennia, we should respect cultures who continue the practice of genocide. How cold. How sad. How misinformed. Please read my blog at https://whaleanddolphintalk.blogspot.com/"

2009/09/09
WcP.Poetic.Thought

We are guests to Earth by chance
we own nothing since birth till death
but owing much to Earth

Guest to Earth by Chance
by LuCxeed

We are guests to Earth by chance
we own nothing since birth till death
but owing much to Universe
to Nature, to Majesty beyond
to Earth
who provide us wealth
air & soil, water & land, food & clothes

we are transient guests
guest by chance to Earth
to whom we're deep in debt
isn't it indubitably simple
isn't it evidently true
as trees are green
the sky blue

Dean Goodluck

www.worldculturepictorial.com/blog/archive/all/2009/09/09

Nature, Universe
Majesty beyond
and Earth
have my worship
as well theirs, those beloved
who lived with generosity, with love
as their once being Earth's guests

Dean Goodluck

2009/09/12
WCP.Humor

*Don't approach a goat from the front,
a horse from the back
or a fool from any side*

"Don't approach a goat from the front,
a horse from the back
or a fool from any side."

"Same trouble, different day."

"Scandal is like an egg;
when it is hatched it has wings."

- Proverbs

www.worldculturepictorial.com/blog/archive/all/2009/09/12

Six Steps Wiser - WcP Reading & Reflection Vol. 06

2009/09/13
WcP.Philosophy

...let the fear of poverty govern your life and your reward will be...

"You are going to let the fear of poverty govern your life and your reward will be that you will eat, but you will not live."
- George Bernard Shaw

www.worldculturepictorial.com/blog/archive/all/2009/09/13

Dean Goodluck

2009/09/15
WCP.Story.Teller

Who did it?
Crop circles

Crop circles, in 1678: Mow'd by Infernal Spirit? No Mortal Man's able to do the like; in 1880: by rainfall, by wind?

www.worldculturepictorial.com/blog/archive/all/2009/09/15

2009/09/17
WcP.Philosophy

We know what we are, but know not what we may be

"We know what we are, but know not what we may be."
- William Shakespeare

www.worldculturepictorial.com/blog/archive/all/2009/09/17

Dean Goodluck

2009/09/19
WCP.Scientific.Mind

Fastest bike by a total unknown

Millions of American R&D dollars chase tail of zero-emissions race motorcycle engineered in India by a total unknown no-money privateer. Cedric Lynch's first electrical motor was made from flattened soup cans; invented a pancake-like-shaped Lynch motor in 1979 and filed relevant patent on 18 December 1986

www.worldculturepictorial.com/blog/archive/all/2009/09/19

Reader Comments

♦ 2009/09/21 – "It seems that the event was exciting and fun for a good cause."

Six Steps Wiser - WcP Reading & Reflection Vol. 06

2009/09/21
WcP.Common.Sense

If we don't end war,
war will end us

"If we don't end war, war will end us."
- Herbert George Wells

www.worldculturepictorial.com/blog/archive/all/2009/09/21

Dean Goodluck

www.worldculturepictorial.com/blog/archive/all/2009/09/23

Six Steps Wiser - WcP Reading & Reflection Vol. 06

2009/09/23
WcP.Tomorrows.History

*Choice for mankind
sharing one planet*

Choice for mankind sharing one planet - where to spend big? To make our only Earth greener, or grayer?

Dean Goodluck

2009/09/25
WCP.Philosophy

*Without courage,
wisdom bears no fruit*

"Without courage, wisdom bears no fruit."
- Baltasar Gracian

www.worldculturepictorial.com/blog/archive/all/2009/09/25

Six Steps Wiser - WcP Reading & Reflection Vol. 06

2009/09/27
WcP.Story.Teller

Verplanck Colvin
Forest Preserve (New York)

Tribute to Verplanck Colvin (1847–1920), pioneer to protect nature. "Woods and Waters" was his 1860 book about his adventures in the Adirondack Mountains. His understanding and appreciation for the environment of the Adirondack Mountains led to the creation of New York's Forest Preserve and the Adirondack Park

www.worldculturepictorial.com/blog/archive/all/2009/09/27

Dean Goodluck

2009/09/29
WCP.Story.Teller

*Makeshift home
napping vendor
overloaded truck*

Makeshift home of old man fleeing from war near mountains, vendor napping by bike full of crafts, overloaded trucks in water: photos

www.worldculturepictorial.com/blog/archive/all/2009/09/29

Reader Comments

♦ 2016/02/19 - "All three images taken in apt time. This shows professionalism of the photography. Old man making home at beautiful mountain view, and the vendor got very good stuff, it's beautiful art. The overloaded bus is really shocking."

♦ 2016/02/18 - "What mind blowing pictures."

Six Steps Wiser - WcP Reading & Reflection Vol. 06

2009/10/01
WcP.Humor

Two things are infinite...

"Two things are infinite:
the universe and human stupidity;
and I'm not sure about the universe."
- Albert Einstein

www.worldculturepictorial.com/blog/archive/all/2009/10/01

Dean Goodluck

2009/10/03
WcP.Observer

What inspires a kiss?

What inspires a kiss? Love, victory, passion, religious devotion, sad farewell... What doesn't? Swine flu.

www.worldculturepictorial.com/blog/archive/all/2009/10/03

Reader Comments

♦ 2016/07/25 - "The thing about kissing anything or anyone is that showing our love towards them. The pictures here shows the different types of kissing. Each picture has different meaning based on their occasion. The meaning of it will change from picture to picture. It is good that people beware of this swine flu and take necessary precautions."

- 2016/07/25 - "Good passion."
- 2016/04/18 - "I had similar doubt of what could have been the reason for kissing the ground or something in their victory. I have noticed many people across the world does this thing as it's shown in the pictures. It was a good article."
- 2010/11/03 - "Nice story! I really appreciate your work! With related pics you've given good news!"
- 2009/10/05 - "Nice post. Kiss expresses love and care. it's our way of showing affection toward our friends, family, and loved ones. nice pictures. thanks for sharing!"

Dean Goodluck

2009/10/05
WCP.Poetic.Thought

sharpness like knife
Shut in upon itself and do no harm
hand of Love, soft and warm
let us hear no sound of human strife

"XXIV - Let the world's sharpness like a clasping knife"
by Elizabeth Barrett Browning
(1806-1861)

Let the world's sharpness like a clasping knife
Shut in upon itself and do no harm
In this close hand of Love, now soft and warm,
And let us hear no sound of human strife
After the click of the shutting. Life to life--
I lean upon thee, Dear, without alarm,
And feel as safe as guarded by a charm
Against the stab of worldlings, who if rife
Are weak to injure. Very whitely still
The lilies of our lives may reassure

Alone to heavenly dews that drop not fewer;
Growing straight, out of man's reach, on the hill.
God only, who made us rich, can make us poor.

www.worldculturepictorial.com/blog/archive/all/2009/10/05

Spend wise –
Guardian to Purse;
waste less –
Angel to Earth.

Six Steps Wiser - WcP Reading & Reflection Vol. 06

2009/10/07
WcP.System.Thinker

Spend wise - Guardian to Purse; waste less - Angel to Earth

"Spend wise - Guardian to Purse; waste less - Angel to Earth." - LuCxeed
Poll: protecting the planet given priority over economy growth. Franklin Roosevelt said in 1937, "we have always known that heedless self-interest was bad morals," in the midst of the Great Depression

www.worldculturepictorial.com/blog/archive/all/2009/10/07

Reader Comments

- 2016/08/28 - "The global warming effect will increase by the usage of plastic and many more. This is a really great thing that many people are interested in buying organic products to save the planet. I have read about the benefits of using organic products."

Dean Goodluck

2009/10/09
WCP.Philosophy

...real tragedy of life...

"We can easily forgive a child
who is afraid of the dark;
the real tragedy of life is
when men are afraid of the light."
- Plato

www.worldculturepictorial.com/blog/archive/all/2009/10/09

Six Steps Wiser - WcP Reading & Reflection Vol. 06

2009/10/11
WcP.System.Thinker

488 hrs of footage shocking aerial shots

No wonder Earth is badly stressed: 488 hours of footage, shocking aerial shots - Earth depleted and destroyed fast and faster - documentary film HOME 2009 covers 50 nations

www.worldculturepictorial.com/blog/archive/all/2009/10/11

Reader Comments

◆ 2018/09/18 - "This is post is amazing. I come to know about the fact regarding nature. Due to the modern lifestyle, we are destroying nature and it is affecting our living planet earth. We have to think and act on it seriously. This documentary opens our eyes. We have to create awareness among people. Everyone has to take initiative for that. We have to read in-depth about this.

Dean Goodluck

2009/10/12
WCP.Poetic.Thought

Your living is determined not so much by what life brings to you as by the attitude you bring to life...

"Your living is determined
not so much by what life brings to you
as by the attitude you bring to life;
not so much by what happens to you
as by the way your mind
looks at what happens."
- Khalil Gibran

www.worldculturepictorial.com/blog/archive/all/2009/10/12

Six Steps Wiser - WcP Reading & Reflection Vol. 06

2009/10/14
WcP.Tomorrows.History

Streets look different on days without my cars!

Merrier and freer on car-free days. "In town without my car!" European Mobility Week in over 2,000 cities and towns

www.worldculturepictorial.com/blog/archive/all/2009/10/14

Dean Goodluck

2009/10/16
WCP.Humor

Q to Planet: "What on Earth's the problem with you?"

Humor and cartoons.
Question to Planet: "What on Earth's the problem with you?"
"hands up"
"sweating turtles"
"fish and fat cat"

www.worldculturepictorial.com/blog/archive/all/2009/10/16

Six Steps Wiser - WcP Reading & Reflection Vol. 06

2009/10/18
WcP.Observer

Maldives underwater cabinet meeting

Republic of Maldives, a small island nation in South Asia with an average ground-level elevation of 1.5m (4ft 11in) above sea level, is the world's lowest-lying country.
Maldives underwater cabinet meeting, chaired by President, took place around a table about 5m (16ft) underwater, and bubbles ascended from the scuba masks

www.worldculturepictorial.com/blog/archive/all/2009/10/18

Dean Goodluck

2009/10/20
WCP.Tomorrows.History

Things alter for the worse spontaneously, if they be not altered for the better designedly

"Things alter for the worse spontaneously, if they be not altered for the better designedly."
- Francis Bacon

www.worldculturepictorial.com/blog/archive/all/2009/10/20

Six Steps Wiser - WcP Reading & Reflection Vol. 06

2009/10/22
WcP.System.Thinker

Ice sheets melting sea rising?

Melting of ice sheets in Greenland and West Antarctica, a 3-foot rise in sea level by 2100?

www.worldculturepictorial.com/blog/archive/all/2009/10/22

Reader Comments

- 2009/10/26 - "A tragedy indeed. We should seriously think on how we can actually help out to have a better environment."
- 2017/06/02 - "We have read so many topics about Boston under water action climate and that makes you happy. That all are much important to find pictorial writing tips. Then everyone will be happy to manage the facts and interesting stories."

Dean Goodluck

2009/10/25
WCP.WatchfulEye

John and Abigail Adams marriage lasted 54 years

25 Oct 1764. Future 2nd US President John Adams (28) weds Abigail Smith (19) in Massachusetts (marriage lasts 54 years)

Political Party: Federalist
Political Titles: Vice President, Member of the Continental Congress, Minister to Great Britain, Minister to the Netherlands

Presidential Term:
March 4, 1797 - March 4, 1801
Preceded By: George Washington
Succeeded By: Thomas Jefferson

www.worldculturepictorial.com/blog/archive/all/2009/10/25

Six Steps Wiser - WcP Reading & Reflection Vol. 06

2009/10/26
WcP.Poetic.Thought

"Good-Night"
by Percy Bysshe Shelley

Good-night? ah! no; the hour is ill
Which severs those it should unite;
Let us remain together still,
Then it will be good night.

How can I call the lone night good,
Though thy sweet wishes wing its flight?
Be it not said, thought, understood --
Then it will be -- good night.

To hearts which near each other move
From evening close to morning light,
The night is good; because, my love,
They never say good-night.

- Good-Night
poem by Percy Bysshe Shelley

www.worldculturepictorial.com/blog/archive/all/2009/10/26

Dean Goodluck

2009/10/28
WCP.Scientific.Mind

Solar-powered car races epic 1864m (3000km) Australia's harshest terrain

Pioneered by the South Australian Tourism Commission, World Solar Challenge 2009 underway: 1,864-mile solar car race across Australia, 38 teams from 17 countries

www.worldculturepictorial.com/blog/archive/all/2009/10/28

Reader Comments

(not in chronological order)
- 2016/05/20 – "This is really nice concept, it surely will work in future."
- 2013/03/28 – "The vehicle looks very innovative and excellent. All have a talent inside their soul, it needs some events to bring out the talent. Like the above vehicle, innovations should be increased day by day."

- 2012/11/02 - "The only problem of these cars is a little energy efficiency. In 10-15 years when the Sun's activity is higher and the technology is improved, this may have sense.
Now this is just a scientists' race.."
- 2012/05/04 - "This type of cars represents the future. For our own health and to reduce air pollution the governement should do all it can to offer us the opportunity to buy these cars. For now I wanna buy a Honda and I wonder what carbon dioxide emission it has."
- 2013/03/16 - "Solar cars are a distant reality. Car makers have yet to realise its full potential of solar power. Technology has to be affordable before it realises."
- 2011/01/05 - "This is nice concept of car race. It will also save fuel and prevent pollution. Now onwards in each and every race we keep solar power energy criteria."
- 2012/04/28 - "I liked the concept, actually same like electric cars we should try to innovate a car that will work on solar and its charge should last long."
- 2011/06/05 - "This is something amazing. Solar car is a good concept, why can't we apply this on our normal running cars it will help to save a lot of fuel."

- 2012/05/02 - "Good idea. I liked the way people are innovating new things, I think we should innovate such kinds of innovation which will take this world to next level."
- 2012/04/30 - "They have promoted very little innovation. The winner is the one with the most expensive solar cells, fanciest lithium battery, most expensive motor and the recipient of the best computer modeling. All of those things already have momentum. How about fostering magination, innovation. That is real engineering."
- 2011/05/03 - "Solar car is an electric car that uses solar energy. This energy is gained from the solar panels called Photovoltaic on the upper surface of the vehicle. These Photovoltaic (PV) cells connect to provide 48-volt battery charge, and they convert sunlight directly into electricity, to power the vehicle."
- 2011/04/10 - "Pretty interesting information. I can't think about solar car racing. It's really an amazing idea. I appreciate this kind of ideas. It's really a nice step for global warming. I hope this prototype Eco-friendly vehicles is available to everyone very soon."

Six Steps Wiser - WcP Reading & Reflection Vol. 06

- 2011/02/22 - "Thanks for sharing this post. This is very helpful and informative material. Good post and keep it up. That's cool stuff, anyways, a good way to get started to renovate your dreams into the world of reality. Thanks."
- 2016/03/27 - "It's like a treat to my eyes to watch the many solar cars at one stop and that too about to compete in he race. This is a good start of emerging technology, where people are very excited for this event. I am happy for these pictures uploaded above."
- 2011/02/18 - "I've been looking for this blog a long time ago. When i saw this solar car I was so impressed and I can't believe that someone can make this. Great. Salute!"
- 2010/06/09 - "Great post. Thanks for taking the time to discuss this, I feel strongly about it and love learning more on this topic. If possible, as you gain expertise, would you mind updating your blog with more information? It is extremely helpful for me."
- 2018/09/21 - "Thank you so much for sharing such superb information with us. Your website is very cool. We are impressed by the details that you have on your site. We Bookmarked this website. Keep it up and again thanks. Regards-"

Dean Goodluck

2009/10/30
WcP.Art

Wily Gaul Asterix and his clumsy friend Obelix

Asterix turns 50: 29 Oct 1959, first adventure of France's hero created by Italian-born artist Uderzo and script-writer Goscinny in Pilote

www.worldculturepictorial.com/blog/archive/all/2009/10/30

Six Steps Wiser - WcP Reading & Reflection Vol. 06

2009/11/01
WcP.Poetic.Thought

Moral excellence comes about as a result of habit...

"Moral excellence comes about
as a result of habit.
We become just by doing just acts,
temperate by doing temperate acts,
brave by doing brave acts."
- Aristotle

www.worldculturepictorial.com/blog/archive/all/2009/11/01

Dean Goodluck

2009/11/03
WCP.Watchful.Eye

Mt. Kilimanjaro
85% of 1912's ice cap gone

Mount Kilimanjaro Ice Cap rapidly retreats, 85% of 1912's ice cover vanished...recent surface melting not occurred over 11,700 yrs

www.worldculturepictorial.com/blog/archive/all/2009/11/03

Reader Comments

- 2010/02/14 – "To think that the snows of Kilimanjaro will vanish in my lifetime... so sad what we have done to this once beautiful planet. Enjoy the little natural beauty that remains, because it wont be around long, I'm not just talking about Kilimanjaro, but simple things like our Mountains (mining blasting the tops off of mountains here in WV), rivers and other landscapes."

Six Steps Wiser - WcP Reading & Reflection Vol. 06

2009/11/05
WcP.Story.Teller

Who is Lewis Gordon Pugh?

Most courageous and greatest swimmer to swim beyond extreme, bearing excruciating pain, not for gold medals but for fragile Nature. Lewis Gordon Pugh said, "we've lost more than half the Arctic summer sea ice cover decades ahead of predictions"

www.worldculturepictorial.com/blog/archive/all/2009/11/05

Reader Comments

♦ 2017/07/31 - "Global population just passed 7 billion and is expected to reach 9.3 billion or more by 2050. 'By the year 2070, we'll live in a hotter world than it's been since humans evolved as a species,' Barnosky said. Increased carbon dioxide in the atmosphere from the burning of fossil fuels is making the ocean more acidic, and less hospitable to sea life."

- 2016/02/03 – "Oh my god I don't know how he's swimming in such frozen sea or lake, it really needs good courage and practice. He has been an extraordinary swimmer which has made him to be in this state."
- 2014/05/16 – "Hi, this is a very interesting article and I have enjoyed reading many of the articles and posts contained on the website, keep up the good work and hope to read some more interesting content in the future. I got a lot of useful and significant information. Thank you so much."

Six Steps Wiser - WcP Reading & Reflection Vol. 06

2009/11/07
WcP.Common.Sense

Canada to withdraw troops anyone left behind?

Canada to withdraw troops from Afghanistan. Photographer's Personal Journey through War: 'hell on earth' 'waiting' 'strays' 'grave'

www.worldculturepictorial.com/blog/archive/all/2009/11/07

Dean Goodluck

2009/11/08
WCP.Tomorrows.History

**8 Nov 1731
Benjamin Franklin opened
first US library**

Before the nineteenth century, books were expensive and rare in North and South America, where there were no public libraries. On 8 Nov 1731, Benjamin Franklin opened the first US library in Philadelphia

www.worldculturepictorial.com/blog/archive/all/2009/11/08

Six Steps Wiser - WcP Reading & Reflection Vol. 06

2009/11/09
WcP.Poetic.Thought

*There's a smile of love
there's a smile of deceit
there's a smile of smiles
in which these two smiles meet...*

The Smile
poem by William Blake

There is a smile of love,
And there is a smile of deceit,
And there is a smile of smiles
In which these two smiles meet.

And there is a frown of hate,
And there is a frown of disdain,
And there is a frown of frowns
Which you strive to forget in vain,

For it sticks in the heart's deep core
And it sticks in the deep backbone--
And no smile that ever was smil'd,
But only one smile alone,

Dean Goodluck

That betwixt the cradle and grave
It only once smil'd can be;
And, when it once is smil'd,
There's an end to all misery.

www.worldculturepictorial.com/blog/archive/all/2009/11/09

Reader Comments

♦ 2010/07/27 – "There is a beautiful song called " eternity in an hour" inspired by Blake's poem. It's worth it to check it out."

Six Steps Wiser - WcP Reading & Reflection Vol. 06

2009/11/11
WcP.Humor

Humor: shoe size 7 vs size 14

Humor and Cartoons:
"I may wear size of 7 shoe, but I leave a size 14..." "truck tires still not a match"

www.worldculturepictorial.com/ blog/ archive/ all/ 2009/11/11

Dean Goodluck

2009/11/12
WCP.Philosophy

*The worst pain a man can suffer:
to have insight into much
and power over nothing*

"The worst pain a man can suffer:
to have insight into much
and power over nothing."
- Herodotus

www.worldculturepictorial.com/blog/archive/all/2009/11/12

Six Steps Wiser - WcP Reading & Reflection Vol. 06

2009/11/14
WcP.Scientific.Mind

Spacecraft onto the Moon to detect water-ice

NASA reveals secrets Moon's been holding for billions of years. Moon is not a dry, desolate place but has water!

www.worldculturepictorial.com/blog/archive/all/2009/11/14

Dean Goodluck

2009/11/16
WCP.System.Thinker

Veggie or meat
Your choice

World Vegan Day and Vegan month: plant-based diet vs meat-eating diet, which way health-wise? Your choice.

www.worldculturepictorial.com/blog/archive/all/2009/11/16

Reader Comments

- 2016/10/10 – "This post is really informative and you have posted such precious and awesome"
- 2014/11/27 – "What a justified analysis! Ah author must be great person..."

- 2010/11/23 - "Very nice post! I would like to read more scientific comparisons between a plant-based diet and animal-based diet. I am still not convinced that animal-based protein is superior (we need to know in what way is animal-based protein more superior)."
- 2010/12/08 - "If you are interested in learning the differences/benefits of plant based protein vs animal based protein I highly recommend 'The China Study'. https://www.amazon.com/China-Study-Comprehensive-Nutrition-Conducted/dp/1574535811
Fantastic book (albeit a bit dry for the first half) that shows that animal proteins are in fact the lower quality proteins and it's the plant proteins that are the high quality proteins. Don't take my word for it, read the book."

Dean Goodluck

2009/11/18
WcP.Observer

Gorbachev to withdraw from counter-productive war

Call to withdraw from "futile and counter-productive war" as former USSR President Gorbachev ended Afghan war in 1988

www.worldculturepictorial.com/blog/archive/all/2009/11/18

Six Steps Wiser - WcP Reading & Reflection Vol. 06

2009/11/20
WcP.Poetic.Thought

Humor is the affectionate communication of insight

"Humor is the affectionate
communication
of insight."
- Leo Rosten

www.worldculturepictorial.com/blog/archive/all/2009/11/20

Dean Goodluck

2009/11/22
WCP.Humor

Mouse keeps chewing ignores leopard's nudge

Tiny vs mighty: hungry African leopard nudges intruder with her nose but mouse keeps chewing on leopard's lunch

www.worldculturepictorial.com/blog/archive/all/2009/11/22

Reader Comments

(not in chronological order)
- 2017/04/21 - "This can be really amusing, the mouse is attempting to eat leopard's food and leopard is looking to save her food. It is like Tom and Jerry story. Ow!! That's a really cute minute. It's a fantastic picture. Affection and the love between creatures is amazing. If people had this kindness within their heart, I wish."

Six Steps Wiser - WcP Reading & Reflection Vol. 06

- 2018/01/30 - "Very beautiful pic shared that show the mercy of animals."
- 2014/03/14 - "It says the leopard has been raised in captivity, so I don't think the leopard has ever had to kill, for food. Thus, the leopard may have lost even the tendency to kill."
- 2014/09/11 - "Not so sure that's what's going on here. My house cats have never had to hunt for food, but they both kill mice whenever they can."
- 2014/04/19 - "My house cats have been raised in captivity, and have NEVER had to hunt. However when they see a rodent they remember how to hunt... Sometimes animals just make unusual friends."
- 2015/12/11 - "Prey is different. Leopards don't hunt mice, they hunt pretty large animals, so I doubt it would have even crossed its mind to waste energy attacking such a pointless morsel. House cats wouldn't hunt an antelope either lol. Also Leopards aren't generally born in places with mice running round, so I'm unsure whether mice would be recognised as prey in the first place. I doubt very much that they've 'made friends' as people keep saying, though, a nudge is not a nuzzle!"
- 2017/10/26 - "It shows that every creature of

- 2012/11/14 - "This is a touching moment. Was he seeing it for the first time? And just was curious what it was? Or he just wanted the mouse to stuff herself with meat? (just joking) I like the pictures! 9 out of 10!"
- 2019/06/07 - "I like your information with good content. Thanks for posting it."
- 2013/04/06 - "Brave rodent? Maybe the mouse was sick. There is a disease that rats sometimes get that cause them to run TOWARDS a predator that they are normally afraid of (e.g., cat, etc.) It is postulated that the virus(?) is causing the brain-sickened rat to become prey in order for the virus to propagate (move into another host, in this case, a cat...) At any rate, this is unusual behavior but not anything 'mystical.' I wouldn't read too much into this other than strangeness but there is an explanation..."
- 2013/08/14 - "Agree."
- 2013/05/28 - "What you're talking about is toxoplasma, which makes rats attracted to the scent of cat pee. I believe it is a parasite, and if you've ever owned a cat and done little box duty, chances are you have it too."
- 2013/06/12 - "The parasite doesn't affect humans though."

- 2013/10/06 - "Untrue. Toxoplasmosis infects a portion of the population, and though you may live life normally unaware of your infection it is not necessarily safe either. Research is being done to understand how toxoplasmosis affects the human body, specifically the nervous system (ex. schizophrenia). Most notably, pregnant women (or rather their fetus) are at the most risk. Sometimes even ending in still births. In all respects, we are finding that parasites, viruses, and bacterial infections can have detrimental effects on a developing child's nervous system and well being."
- 2013/04/26 - "Dude. It's sweet. Just go with it. Don't need to explain everything."
- 2013/10/23 - ":D totally man, it's amazing no matter what the reason."
- 2016/04/11 - "Those pictures are really fascinating to watch. I can see the defenselessness in leopard's eyes with the brave attack of tiny mouse on the food of leopard. Leopard is kind enough to allow this tiny guest to share her meal. The photography was superb with great timing. The articles were written in a funny way."
- 2015/09/03 - "It's interesting to read but afraid to watch."

- 2017/03/23 - "Friends will be friends! I can understand most people don't have any emotional attachment to their best friends, but some friends actually value their best friend. They know the important of such person in their life. These pictures are just awesome, 10 out of 10! I personally have also one person who I can call myself best friends. We help each other in almost everything, discuss our issues etc. We even supported each other in semester's exams."
- 2017/04/18 - "It's really amazing but that is also the example of love among both of them."
- 2010/04/16 - "It's very cool... That is the real essence of friendship. Even though they are different in ways but they make still friends... Mouse is Stronger than Sheena. lol.."
- 2013/09/07 - "Well... The only problem with stories like this is that people humanize them too much. In a lot of these cases of predator 'befriending' prey the predator will eventually turn on the other animal. The most likely situation for this photo is that the cat prefers the meat chunks to the mouse and if it was hungry and the meat chunks weren't there it would definitely kill the mouse."

- 2018/07/04 – "Great animals you have in this article."
- 2018/07/04 – "Thank You for such a good article, the picture of animals is really amazing."
- 2017/10/26 – "It's more than amazing. How a monster cares for the tiny. I'm really impressed. Everything has sense."
- 2016/03/01 – "Must appreciate the timing of the photographer who captured the most amazing moments between the leopard and the mouse. This is so funny, the mouse is trying to eat leopard's food and leopard is trying to save her food. So funny... it's like a Tom and Jerry tale."
- 2017/12/15 – "This is really something very interesting."
- 2017/12/11 – "Take every chance you get in life, because some things only happen once."
- 2017/05/16 – "Nice article. I am eagerly waiting for your next article. This is more interesting. I would like to say thanks for sharing this."
- 2014/05/30 – "Wow!! That is really a cute moment. It is an amazing photograph. The love and affection between animals is unbelievable. I wish if human had this kindness in their heart.

Dean Goodluck

- 2016/01/12 - "This photography of Casey Gutteridge is of excellent quality. The pictures has good resolutions in it which is able to show everything clearly about leopard and mouse. The author wrote the article in very funny way and plays between leopard and mouse which is eating the meal of leopard in front of him without caring about the leopard."
- 2016/08/10 - "Great picture. I like everything here."
- 2018/11/15 - "Wow... The photograph is very nice. First I didn't notice the rat in the picture then closely watched them all."
- 2019/06/07 - "I like your information with good content. Thanks for posting it."
- 2018/11/15 - "Nice blog. I am really happy with your blog because your article is very unique and powerful for new readers. Thank you for sharing informative article with us...nice post"
- 2019/06/09 - "Your article is very interesting and fantastic, at the same time the theme is unique and perfect, great job."
- 2017/08/11 - "High quality information, useful, thanks."
- 2013/04/26 - "Interesting. Thanks for sharing."
- 2017/09/08 - "I need to thank you for your chance for this awesome read!!"

Six Steps Wiser - WcP Reading & Reflection Vol. 06

- 2016/10/15 - "Nice. You're so interesting! I do not think I have read through something like that before. So wonderful to discover somebody with a few unique thoughts on this subject matter. Really... Many thanks for starting this up. This site is something that is required on the internet, someone with a little originality!"
- 2018/10/20 - "I really like and appreciate your work. I read deeply your article, the points you have mentioned in this article are useful."
- 2018/05/09 - "Thank you for sharing excellent information. Your website is very cool. I am impressed by the details that you have on this blog. It reveals how nicely you understand this subject."
- 2017/06/18 - "I was amazed by you. The way you create a website is very thorough and good. This is very very impressive. Thank you for sharing, and hopefully more successful."
- 2017/05/23 - "By the way, thank you for sharing with us, and we sincerely hope you will continue to update or post other articles.
- 2016/10/15 - "This is the first time that I visit here. This is a site with great enlightening blogs, good user boundary, clean and pleasant. I will be back soon, thanks for the great blog.""

Dean Goodluck

2009/11/24
WCP.System.Thinker

Annual loss
273 gigatons of water

The math: if one gigaton could provide enough water for 17 million, then 273 gigatons? Greenland ice melting 3 times faster, loss of vast ice sheet and weight affecting Earth gravitational pull, 273 gigatons of water now pouring into oceans annually

www.worldculturepictorial.com/blog/archive/all/2009/11/24

Reader Comments

♦ 2014/11/18 – "The developed country should come first to reduce the effect of melting ice, otherwise the low geographical countries will be submerged."

Six Steps Wiser - WcP Reading & Reflection Vol. 06

2009/11/26
WcP.Common.Sense

*Regret is insight
that comes a day too late*

"Regret is insight
that comes a day too late."
- Northrop Frye

www.worldculturepictorial.com/blog/archive/all/2009/11/26

Dean Goodluck

2009/11/28
WCP.Watchful.Eye

Dubai catching up debt, and solar panels

2009: $59-billion debt; endless sun, but no solar panels. What kind of modernity?
2016: plans world's largest solar project
2019: $124-billion debt, ready to take on more if needed

www.worldculturepictorial.com/blog/archive/all/2009/11/28

Reader Comments

- 2010/05/02 – "It looks just like a big, greedy, ugly monster, ready to cut open the sky."
- 2018/02/02 – "I expect to see more from you in the future with nice information like this one."

Six Steps Wiser - WcP Reading & Reflection Vol. 06

2009/11/30
wcP.life.Coach

Spain, Italy, Germany, UK, France ban "too-thin" Models

Fashion, health and beauty in real life get along? Spain banned skinny models in 2006. So does Germany's Brigitte

Who else?
2006 Spain, Germany and Italy ban "too-thin" models
2012 Vogue bans too-skinny models from its pages
　　　Too young and too thin is no longer in
2015 France votes to ban ultra-thin models in crackdown on anorexia
2016 UK bans Gucci ad for "unhealthily thin" model
2017 French fashion giants ban super-skinny models from catwalks
2017 France's ban on unhealthily thin models officially in effect with law requiring doctor's certificate

Dean Goodluck

World Health Organisation adult BMI
underweight: below 18.5
severely malnourished: below 17
anorexia? 16 is the measure of an average model

www.worldculturepictorial.com/blog/archive/all/2009/11/30

Reader Comments

(not in chronological order)
♦ 2018/07/07 - "One of Spain's most lofty design demonstrates has consented to prohibit excessively thin models from participating. The coordinators of Madrid Fashion Week are utilizing the Weight File - a count in light of tallness and weight - to dismiss models that are too thin."

Six Steps Wiser - WeP Reading & Reflection Vol. 06

◆ 2012/10/09 - "'skinny' or just 'thin'?

I both disagree and agree with all this. Yes, skinny models are beautiful to look at inspiring both a loathing passion of jealousy and a need to be exactly like them (only better), but then again 'real' women as was said in this article inspire readers and viewers to RELATE to them.

These 'real' women, these 'curvy' woman are really no different from skinny models.

Admit it we all want to be 'a little thinner' to fit into those old jeans from those younger days or that cute new size 4 at the local dress store. Whats different about these unhealthily skinny models is that they took something to the extreme because they believed they weren't pretty enough or they were to fat.

Believe it or not while it was there dissuasion as a person to 'starve themselves' it our fault as a society for goading this on.

Dean Goodluck

We all are looking for that 'perfect' model whether to envy or dream of being or pick out their flaws and when faced with this amazing 'new' idea of 'real' women it's the exact thing with a different pair of eyes.

The idea of always being 'too fat' will remain in the brain to contaminate the confidence of a persons natural 'healthy' build and maybe eventually win over the model. We see this all the time in celebrities.

They tell the press they're happy to be curvaceous then turn around and start losing weight out the wazzoo because they got insecure.

It's really not their fault they feel this way, I think in a way we all think the same, its none of anybody's fault but our own, because we as a group decided for the rest of the world what was 'beautiful' and what was not.

Don't believe me? Look at the facts staring you in the face, models and people like celebrities ESPECIALLY women will always be subjected to this unfortunate insecurity of 'being to big' and the readers will pretend not to see and think 'maybe it's natural' and continue with their lives like nothings happened.

The readers will always want the skinnier model because in our mind we hope one day we can be LIKE them, it's the plain awful truth... and don't give me crap about you 'not caring about this kind of thing', you do. We all do. Even if it is unconscious."
- ◆ 2018/05/15 - "Germany's most well-known ladies' magazine is restricting proficient models from its pages and supplanting them with pictures of 'genuine living' ladies."
- ◆ 2018/04/10 - "This is really awesome design, this is especially a fashion of younger generation of Spanish women."
- ◆ 2017/11/17 - "Skinny models should be discouraged as they don't look good and set a wrong example on the normal girls who try to copy anything the celebrities do."

- 2018/05/04 - "Everyone is aware of the health issues caused by obesity. But being too skinny also has severe effects on your health."
- 2017/12/08 - "Germany has done a very good thing in favor of all the women out there in imposing this ban on skinny models. I think more countries should impose the same ban to encourage women to eat healthy and stay healthy. Skinny models are only skinny because they are not eating right."
- 2018/06/06 - "It's not healthy if too skinny. You can buy waist trainers for yourself if you want a flat belly."
- 2019/11/26 - "Germany and Spain both are on the same trend by banning skinny models. This decision has both positive and negative impact. Lot of people will go unemployed."
- 2018/04/26 - "I don't like skinny people at all. Neither is obesity good neither is being thin a good sign. I think a person should eat healthy, exercise daily and keep a moderate outlook towards life. This is the best path."
- 2017/12/12 - "I think skinny models don't look good so what is the point in being skinny. A model should neither fat nor skinny."

- 2017/09/09 - "I support the ban. I think it's a good thing that Germany is banning skinny models. It will gradually develop a healthy lifestyle among the young generation who is currently obsessed with extreme dieting and skinny figures."
- 2017/09/05 - "Fashion is my passion, and I respect the creativity that you find in its different levels."
- 2017/07/06 - "This is fantastic collection of fashion styles, thank you for sharing."
- 2017/03/25 - "Skinny models do look good on the ramp but overly skinny seems weird, I have written about different women willing to do some dieting but I guess none means like those models. I am pleased to see that the health ministry has banned them to go for model run. Thanks for the incredible share."
- 2016/03/21 - "If these models continue to appear of magazine covers, or on popular fashion events then it would send a wrong message to the young girls. However, most designers these days prefer launching their collection online."

- 2016/03/21 - "Fashion has a huge impact on people's life, especially those skinny models we see on the catwalk, wearing fancy outfits. No one should go that far just to look like them. We can keep up with the trends and stay healthy at the same time. No one should starve themselves, just to fit into some skinny clothes."
- 2016/03/18 - "Unhealthy fashion trends like this should be banned from every single fashion event."
- 2016/03/18 - "Fashion trends like this should be banned everywhere because these create a negative impact on people. However, it is best to not follow any kind of fashion trend blindly. Just have some classy, timeless pieces in your wardrobe along with a couple of personsalized leather belts."
- 2015/02/06 - "Fashion is very short term trend, during winters people are follow their hero and favorite style with colour."
- 2017/12/19 - "I completely agree with the fact that being thin or thick has nothing to do with looking beautiful. Spain banning skinny models is something I admire and appreciate very much, and I'm going to do my essay on this subject."

Six Steps Wiser - WcP Reading & Reflection Vol. 06

- 2018/06/06 - "These models are so fashionable but too skinny. I'm sure you will change your weight loss methods."
- 2013/01/27 - "Poor things. This is sad. These women feel the need to disfigure there body and slowly kill themselves to live up to what media defines as beauty. I know people say that ugly people say that beauty comes from within, but not to brag I am attractive out and in and I am implying it. For these women they have made there body look like a cadaver that is barely alive. I am sure they are beautiful in the inside because like obese people they are no different. I think I would rather be obese than look as sick as these potentially beautiful women."
- 2018/10/15 - "Great topic. In the above post, all the photo of mold and polished outfits are overgenerous and marvelous. You completed a great and astounding employment to demonstrate these sorts of online journals and posts."
- 2011/11/17 - "I think skinny models do not look nice. I think it is right that Spain bans skinny models. Those who live in Barcelona apartments may like to read this article."
- 2016/03/31 - "You always write in favor of positive things and only look the genuine quality. Marvelous concept!"

Dean Goodluck

♦ 2014/07/02 – "Style Suggestions and Tips

Have you pushed trend to the back burner? There is nothing at all improper with that. It really is in no way as well late to deliver to life your feeling of design.

You need to not acquire an product just because it is on sale at a excellent value. If this doesn't function with your human body fashion or it is still a bit out of your finances, it may possibly not be value it right after all. If it's not a thing that's flattering and a thing you adore, it's going to obtain dust in your closet.

Black and white, a extremely popular combination, is in once again this season. There are several outfits on the runway that use this mixture. You can quickly include the colors into your outfits, such as pairing a white shirt with black trousers or sporting a black and white costume. There are an infinite quantity of combos that can be created with black and white.

Just mainly because a trend craze is well-liked does not suggest it will be correct for you. You might appear foolish in the same outfit that seems to be fantastic on the model strolling down the runway. Create your very own style and avoid slipping for supposedly hot trends offered in vogue magazines that expire quicker than a gallon of milk. Trust in your individual instincts. You will not be led down the erroneous path.

You want to have a first rate sum, but not significantly makeup with you. Think about your desires for working day and night purposes. Makeup will not last forever once it is opened. Germs can even improve on it if it is just sitting there.

There are people who imagine that trend just suggests clothes. Your hair can simply wreck an outfit if it's not seeking its best. Get a reduce that is flattering and manageable, and spend in hair products and accessories that support you obtain a glance that meshes properly with your personal model.

Hold an eye out for the sizes of outfits. This implies that, no make a difference what it is, you want to try it on prior to purchasing it. Sizes are no longer centered on set measurements. Some models have quite different dimensions from another. When you purchase outfits on-line, meticulously review the web site's sizing chart. Uncover out their return policy as well."

- 2018/02/01 - "Great post, I read many articles on fashion but never got such nice post on fashion."
- 2018/05/24 - "I am happy someone decided to sooner or later clear things up on this. I have thought about it many times before. :)"
- 2018/05/16 - "Great Job! Keep sharing such wonderful posts."
- 2017/11/10 - "I thank you for the information! I was looking for and could not find. You helped me! Thank you for your work on the blog! You're doing a good job!"

Six Steps Wiser - WcP Reading & Reflection Vol. 06

2009/12/02
WcP.life.Coach

Nothing will benefit human health and increase the chances for survival of life on earth...

"Nothing will benefit human health and increase the chances for survival of life on earth as much as the evolution to a vegetarian diet."
- Albert Einstein

www.worldculturepictorial.com/blog/archive/all/2009/12/02

Dean Goodluck

2009/12/03
WCP.Tomorrows.History

*Brooklyn Bridge
world 1st steel suspension bridge
opened in 1883*

Building and painting Brooklyn Bridge, world's first steel suspension bridge, 5,989 feet long, began in 1869, opened in 1883

www.worldculturepictorial.com/blog/archive/all/2009/12/03

Reader Comments

♦ 2019/08/30 - "Nice to see this beautiful blog! Please keep sharing such type of Information with us. Looking forward from your side."

2009/12/04
WcP.System.Thinker

Brilliant! Costa Rica planted 6.5 million trees $0 on military

Leader's vision and commitment. Oscar Arias and Costa Rica: planted 6.5 million trees by 2007 while spending $0 on military

www.worldculturepictorial.com/blog/archive/all/2009/12/04

Dean Goodluck

2009/12/05
WCP.Philosophy

Mountains are earth's undecaying monuments

"Mountains are earth's undecaying monuments."
- Nathaniel Hawthorne

www.worldculturepictorial.com/blog/archive/all/2009/12/05

Six Steps Wiser - WcP Reading & Reflection Vol. 06

2009/12/06
WcP.Watchful.Eye

Nepal
Cabinet meeting at Mt. Everest

Nepal: world highest Cabinet meeting at Everest
Himalayan glaciers retreating fast, will they disappear?

www.worldculturepictorial.com/blog/archive/all/2009/12/06

Reader Comments

♦ 2017/10/10 - "There are different glaciers in the world which are very huge in the height and very much dangerous. There are different people who want to take tour of such glaciers of the world. Accordingly you can watch these type of glaciers on your devices."

Dean Goodluck

www.worldculturepictorial.com/blog/archive/all/2009/12/07

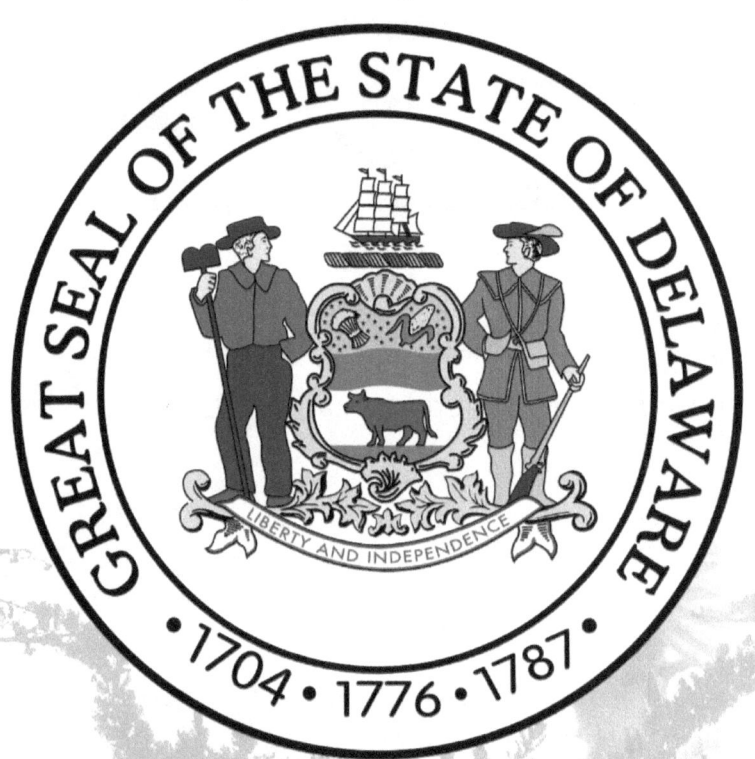

Six Steps Wiser - WcP Reading & Reflection Vol. 06

2009/12/07
WcP.Tomorrows.History

7 Dec 1787
Delaware
first state of US

On 7 Dec 1787, Delaware became the first of the original 13 US states
Motto: "Liberty and Independence"
Anthem: "Our Delaware" (words by George B. Hynson and Donn Devine, music by Will M. S. Brown, based on original poem by Hynson)

www.worldculturepictorial.com/blog/archive/all/2009/12/07

Dean Goodluck

2009/12/09
WCP.Common.Sense

Shared blue seas free dumpster?

Oil leak, marine debris, toxic dumping, mercury tripled. Shocking photos, ocean polluted. Man-made disaster or nature's "myth"?

www.worldculturepictorial.com/blog/archive/all/2009/12/09

Reader Comments

(not in chronological order)
- 2018/05/24 - "OMG it's terrible. I'm sure environment pollution is the world's number one problem. These photos make me angry."
- 2017/10/23 - "It's amazing how much this planet can sustain, why do we allow such pollution in exchange for money and profits? I just don't understand. Poor animals."

Six Steps Wiser - WcP Reading & Reflection Vol. 06

- 2016/06/01 - "A big part of pollution is manmade and there is only a small portion made by nature. We the people pollute our nation in various ways and finally we all have to face such issues. Thank you for sharing the article and keep sharing such things."
- 2017/09/22 - "These pictures are really shocking. By looking at these I felt very bad that I am also one of the participants in destroying nature by our daily used harmful items in this world. I would like to start writing an article about this damage that we all are doing to Mother Nature."
- 2016/04/29 - "People are very much aware of such pollution and again we are polluting our environment. Chemical waste from industries and other areas are dumped in sea and this is a major reason for such ocean pollution."
- 2017/05/02 - "Yes, it is an informative article. We should clean our water because there are many animals died because of this."
- 2018/04/22 - "Very helpful advice in this particular post! It's the little changes that make the largest changes."

- 2016/04/13 - "Nowadays there are huge amounts of pollutants that cause severe environmental problems. The picture shows ocean pollution and it may be because of oils, toxic materials and ocean dumping etc. this is not a nature's myth but surely man made disaster."
- 2016/02/19 - "With all the efforts made by non-governmental organizations and environmentalists, the level of pollution is still increasing. Given this situation, most people often rely on groundwater surveyors to undergo inspections on their properties, in order to supply the water consumption from their own resources. We must be more careful than ever."
- 2018/03/23 - "The problem of global warming is at the present time and if a large number of articles tell about this, then the problem becomes more global with each month. The problem of politicians is nonlinear thinking and the pursuit of one's goals and desires."
- 2017/01/12 - "Very important article. There is alot of food for thought. Thanks for sharing."

Six Steps Wiser - WcP Reading & Reflection Vol. 06

2009/12/11
WcP.Watchful.Eye

Price to boom economy sneezing and coughing in air

As Danish proverb goes, fresh air impoverishes doctors. It's luxury you have when you're breathing, inhaling air as fresh as before. 7 major pollutants in air pollution

www.worldculturepictorial.com/blog/archive/all/2009/12/11

Reader Comments

(not in chronological order)
- 2019/04/18 – "SOS – We must be careful about our environment. Soon we will not be able to breathe in some places of the world, because the pollution is increasing."
- 2017/05/27 – "Unfortunately, we have to face the sad reality that the world we know is disappearing because of human pollution."

- 2016/10/01 – "The environment is very important, try to think if the air, contaminated water, people will live, the only thing you do not know what to think ahead to the future, let's protect the environment for our children and grandchildren."
- 2012/02/11 – "Pollution has become a serious problem, if we ignore it and continue to pollute the environment will occur ecological disaster."
- 2017/10/25 – "Maybe the next 20 years, to get clean air, to be something expensive, and the price of the air conditioner (AC) may be 10 times that of now, and humans are willing to pay it, just to get clean air."
- 2017/08/17 – "Humans cannot appreciate nature. So I think if human behavior is still like that and do not want to change. Do not blame if nature avenge and give disaster."
- 2013/07/04 – "Pollution, What Will We Do? It is so scary to think that in the future, air pollution would be so big that it greatly impacts the lives of people here on Earth. If this kind of pollution can't be stopped at all costs, who knows what will become of Mother Earth by then? We only read it on the research paper and newspapers, but don't you think about it sometimes?"

- 2010/05/05 - "If we ignore and continue to pollute our air. This is not the only worst thing that will happen to us."
- 2012/07/16 - "Pollution is a major problem that affects the environment and people's health. It is caused especially by cars and it can be reduced if people would think in other transport means such as public transport or bycicle. I've recently decided to give my car to an auto donations center and to buy a bycicle instead as in this way I respect the environment. Moreover it is cheaper as I don't have to pay anymore for gas."
- 2017/08/26 - "That is a great idea to show the relevancies."
- 2019/01/08 - "The article tells us about the earth is important for human life. So we should be careful about our environment pollution."
- 2010/09/27 - "Pure air is only dream for our children."
- 2011/02/16 - "Pollution has become a major problem in today's times. With the ever increasing levels of pollution it really scares me to think what our earth will be like some years down the line. Everyone should take it upon themselves to contribute towards reducing pollution in their little possible ways."

- 2010/04/10 - "There should be proper guided steps to make sure that the emissions are minimal and that not too toxic for the earth to breathe. There is a lot of factory waste in the air and water in large quantities which has to be considered... We can also do our small steps by cleaning the emissions of AC and car."
- 2015/09/03 - "Pollution is one of the dangerous factors that lead to the destruction of the earth and also the reasons for many serious diseases. Air pollution increases the rate of pollution. Keep updating such post!"
- 2015/08/24 - "Interesting topic for a blog. I have been searching the Internet for fun and came upon your website. Fabulous post. Thanks a ton for sharing your knowledge! It is great to see that some people still put in an effort into managing their websites. I'll be sure to check back again real soon."
- 2011/03/04 - "The catchy blog with the interesting contents. You give nice information that many people don't know before. Most of your contents make me have more knowledge. It is very different. I was impressed with your blog. Never be bored to visit your website again. Have a nice day. Enjoyed your blogging."

Six Steps Wiser - WcP Reading & Reflection Vol. 06

2009/12/12
WcP.Story.Teller

Ocean guardians. Earthrace joins Sea Shepherd fleet to save whales

A world record. The 100% biofuel fiberglass eco-boat, Earthrace (founder/skipper New Zealander Pete Bethune), traveled 23,497 nautical miles, through Panama and Suez Canals, took 60 days 23 hours 49 mins (1,463 hours, 49 minutes) finishing back in Spain, crossing the finish line on 27 June 2008

www.worldculturepictorial.com/blog/archive/all/2009/12/12

Dean Goodluck

2009/12/13
WCP.Life.Coach

A human being is a part of a whole, called by us 'universe'...

"A human being is a part of a whole,
called by us 'universe',
a part limited in time and space.
He experiences himself,
his thoughts and feelings
as something separated from the rest...
a kind of optical delusion
of his consciousness.
This delusion is a kind of prison for us,
restricting us to our personal desires and
to affection for a few persons nearest to us.
Our task must be to free ourselves from
this prison by widening our circle of
compassion to embrace all living creatures
and the whole of nature in its beauty."
- Albert Einstein

www.worldculturepictorial.com/blog/archive/all/2009/12/13

Six Steps Wiser - WcP Reading & Reflection Vol. 06

2009/12/15
WcP.Observer

Bargain with Nature or remake Nature's law?

Sounds too simple to be true. Earth does not bargain but simply reacts to whatever is "dumped" into the air, into the sea, onto the land, washed by rain into the water

www.worldculturepictorial.com/blog/archive/all/2009/12/15

Dean Goodluck

www.worldculturepictorial.com/blog/archive/all/2009/12/18

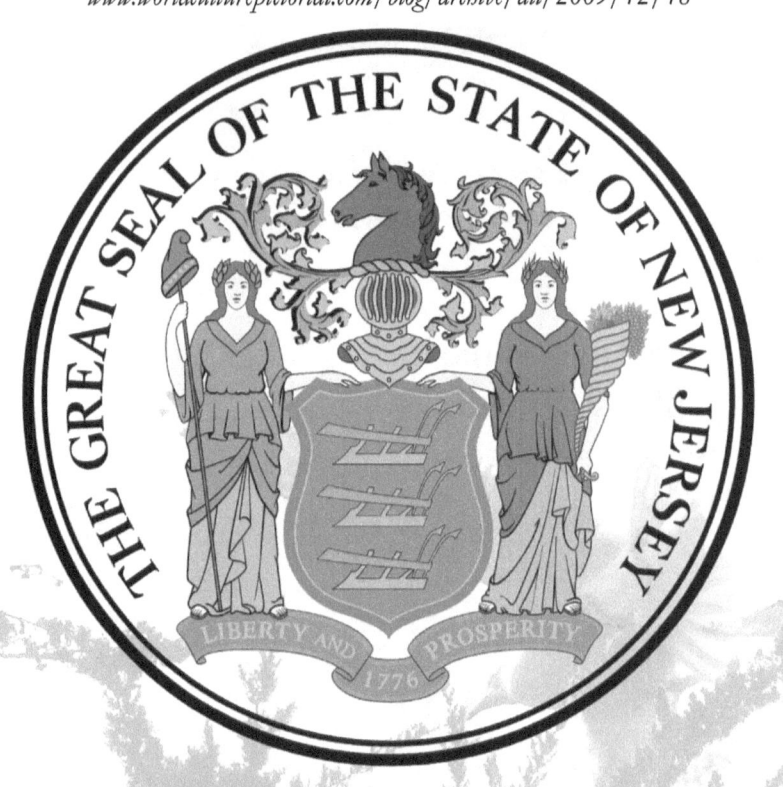

Six Steps Wiser - WcP Reading & Reflection Vol. 06

2009/12/18
WcP.Tomorrows.History

7 Dec 1787
Third state of US

New Jersey (nickname: "The Garden State") became the third of the original 13 US states on 18 Dec 1787 with motto "Liberty and Prosperity" embedded on its state seal.
Inhabited by Native Americans for over 2,800 years (with historical tribes such as the Lenape), the first European settlements were made by the Dutch and the Swedes in the early 17th century, later seized by the English

Dean Goodluck

2009/12/19
WCP.Poetic.Thought

Ring out the old, ring in the new,
Ring, happy bells, across the snow...

"Ring out the old, ring in the new,
Ring, happy bells, across the snow:
The year is going, let him go;
Ring out the false, ring in the true."
- Alfred Lord Tennyson

www.worldculturepictorial.com/blog/archive/all/2009/12/19

Six Steps Wiser - WcP Reading & Reflection Vol. 06

2009/12/20
WcP.Humor

Snow fails no one
Ho ho ho, happy holidays!

Santa Claus running in blizzard;
White Christmas in London;
skis in Capitol Hill;
snow-covered Great Wall.
Would you expect more?

www.worldculturepictorial.com/blog/archive/all/2009/12/20

Dean Goodluck

2009/12/22
WCP.Scientific.Mind

Bertrand Piccard, pilot, aeronaut
André Borschberg, pilot, balloonist
Swiss plane: Solar Impulse

Smashing record! "No frills"! Just as Albert Einstein said, "when the solution is simple, God is answering". Wide as a jumbo jet but weighing just 1,500kg, first of its kind solar plane, Airbus-sized, flies around the world without fuel in prototype runway debut

www.worldculturepictorial.com/blog/archive/all/2009/12/22

Reader Comments

◆ 2012/12/08 - "This is great. I wonder if they will use a similar mechanism for the cars. I will definitely change my car. It's very important to protect the environement and the solar power is a perfect solution."

- 2013/07/29 - "Yes that would be awesome. If something like this works on cars, then we could all celebrate."
- 2013/08/20 - "Great invention! The speed of only 70 km/h isn't very impressive but that wasn't the aim! I admire green environmentally safe inventions! I adore fully-electric vehicles and this solar power plane is also adorable!"
- 2014/03/05 - "While we have oil owners wanting millions, all kinds of alternative energy is out of law."

Dean Goodluck

Six Steps Wiser - WcP Reading & Reflection Vol. 06

2009/12/24
WcP.Publisher

ThinkAhead™ Calendar 2010 series to Health of Earth: ice, forest and ocean. Happy Holidays to all!

"In dwelling, live close to the ground. In thinking, keep to the simple."
- Lao Tzu

www.worldculturepictorial.com/blog/archive/all/2009/12/24

Reader Comments

♦ 2016/09/12 - "Humans are not the ones to think ahead about the well-being of nature. Our climate is changing drastically and the environment is becoming less friendly for humans. All these calendars and efforts are a waste before our greed to earn money."

Dean Goodluck

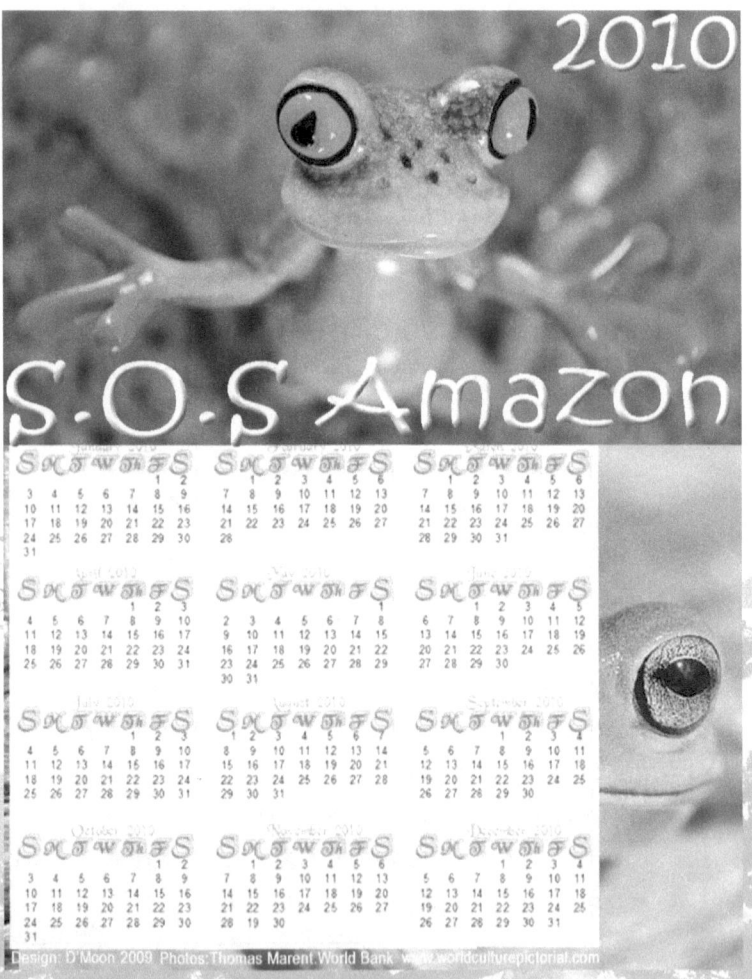

Six Steps Wiser - WcP Reading & Reflection Vol. 06

2009/12/24
WcP.Publisher

I think, therefore I am

"Cogito ergo sum.
(I think, therefore I am.)"
- René Descartes

www.worldculturepictorial.com/blog/archive/all/2009/12/24

Dean Goodluck

Six Steps Wiser - WcP Reading & Reflection Vol. 06

2009/12/24
WcP.Publisher

*Happiness is when what you think,
what you say,
and what you do are in harmony*

"Happiness is when what you think, what you say, and what you do are in harmony."
- Mahatma Gandhi

www.worldculturepictorial.com/ blog/ archive/ all/ 2009/ 12/ 24

Dean Goodluck

2009/12/26
WcP.Story.Teller

"Robin Hood banker"

At cost of her own, a German banker helped the poor from losing their homes, moving millions of euros to prevent people's accounts closing due to financial crisis. Some customers were unable to pay their debts at all. The banker has to pay the bank for the loss (1.1 million euros, £991,000) through her pension, and is given a 22-month suspended jail term

www.worldculturepictorial.com/ blog/ archive/ all/ 2009/ 12/ 26

2009/12/28
WcP.Observer

Discovery Channel
"Whale Wars 2"
Most courageous volunteers

Blue whale, the giant marine mammal, is the largest known creature that has ever lived, at 29.9m (98 ft) and 190 metric tons. Baleen whales and toothed whales are believed to have split apart around 34 million years ago. So to speak, hard not to respect them as Ocean Gods, and the southern ocean as their sanctuary protected by international law. Imagine bravest vulunteers standing between 750-ton whale-killing machine with military-class LRADs and its prey to defend the gentle yet defenseless ocean giants

www.worldculturepictorial.com/blog/archive/all/2009/12/28

Dean Goodluck

2009/12/30
WCP.Poetic.Thought

Tonight
"Blue Moon"
2nd Full Moon within a month

Take a moment to look into Nature, into Future. Blue Moon will watch over New Year celebrations and deer may drop by for a visit

www.worldculturepictorial.com/blog/archive/all/2009/12/30

Six Steps Wiser - WcP Reading & Reflection Vol. 06

...uis Stevenson

"Wine is bottled poetry"

Dean Goodluck

The Grand Consulation

Six Steps Wiser - WcP Reading & Reflection Vol. 06

Poem
The Grand Consulation
George Canning

"Ambubaiarum Collegia Pharmacopeiæ."
-- Horace

If the health and the strength,
    and the pure vital breath
Of old England, at last must be doctor'd to death,
Oh! why must we die of one doctor alone?
And why must that doctor be just such a one
As Doctor Henry Addington?

Oh! where is the great Doctor Dominicetti,
With his stews and his flues,
    and his vapours to sweat ye?
O! where is that Prince of all Mountebank fame,
With his baths of hot earth, and his beds of hot name.
Oh! where is Doctor Graham?

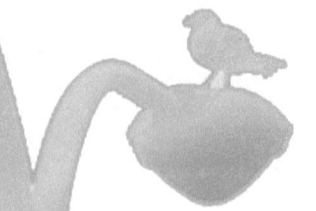

Dean Goodluck

Where are Sonmambule Mesmer's
    convulsions magnetic?
Where is Myersbach, renown'd for his skills diuretic
Where is Perkins, with tractors of magical skill?
Where's the anodyne necklace of Basil Burchell?
Oh! where is the great Van Butchell?

Where's Sangrado Rush, so notorious for bleedings;
Where's Rumford, so famed
    for his writings and readings;
Where's that Count of the Kettle,
    that friend to the belly,
So renown'd for transforming old bones into jelly--
Where, too, is the great Doctor Kelly?

Six Steps Wiser - WeP Reading & Reflection Vol. 06

While Sam Solomon's lotion the public absterges,
He gives them his gold as well as his purges;
But our frugal doctor this practice to shun,
Gives his pills to the public, the Pells to his Son
Oh! fie! fie! Doctor Addington!
Oh! where is Doctor Solomon?

Where are all the great Doctors? No longer we want
This farrago of cowardice, cunning and cant,
These braggarts! that one moment
    know not what fear is,
And the next moment, trembling,
    no longer know where is--
Lord Hawkesbury's march to Paris?

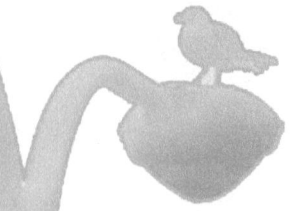

Dean Goodluck

Then for Hobart and Sullivan,
    Hawkey and Hervey,
For Wallace and Castlereagh,
    Bleeke and Glenbervie,
For Sergeant, Vansittart, Monkhouse, and Lee,
Gives us Velno and Anderson, Locke, Spilsbury,
Doctor Ball, Doctors Brodum and Bree.

And instead of the jack-pudding bluster of Sherry,
With his "dagger of lath," and his speeches so
merry!
Let us bring to the field--every foe to appal--
Aldini's galvanic deceptions--and all
The slight of hand tricks of Conjuror Val.

Six Steps Wiser - WcP Reading & Reflection Vol. 06

So shall Golding and Bond, the Doctor's tall yeomen,
Dame Hiley, Dame Bragge,
    and the other old Women,
For new mountebanks changed,
    their old tricks bid farewell to,
And to the famed D'Ivernois his arithmetic sell to,
That wonderful wonder, the great Katterfelto!

So shall England, escaped from her "safe politicians,"
Such an army array of her quacks and physicians,
Such lotions and potions, pills, lancets, and leeches,
That Massena shall tremble our coasts
    when he reaches,
And the Consul himself--his breeches.

- The Grand Consulation
by George Canning

Dean Goodluck

Poem
Half-Waking
William Allingham

I thought it was the little bed
I slept in long ago;
A straight white curtain at the head,
And two smooth knobs below.
I thought I saw the nursery fire,
And in a chair well-known
My mother sat, and did not tire
With reading all alone.
If I should make the slightest sound
To show that I'm awake,
She'd rise, and lap the blankets round,
My pillow softly shake;
Kiss me, and turn my face to see
The shadows on the wall,
And then sing Rousseau's Dream to me,
Till fast asleep I fall.
But this is not my little bed;
That time is far away;
With strangers now I live instead,
From dreary day to day.

- Half-Waking
by William Allingham

Dean Goodluck

In Memoriam (Easter 1995)

Six Steps Wiser - WcP Reading & Reflection Vol. 06

Poem
In Memoriam
(Easter, 1915)
Edward Thomas

The flowers left thick at nightfall in the wood
This Eastertide call into mind the men,
Now far from home, who,
    with their sweethearts, should
Have gathered them and will do never again.

- In Memoriam
by Edward Thomas

Dean Goodluck

Paradise Lost

Six Steps Wiser - WcP Reading & Reflection Vol. 06

Poem
Paradise Lost: Book 02
(lines 1-154)
John Milton

High on a throne of royal state, which far
Outshone the wealth or Ormus and of Ind,
Or where the gorgeous East with richest hand
Showers on her kings barbaric pearl and gold,
Satan exalted sat, by merit raised
To that bad eminence; and, from despair
Thus high uplifted beyond hope, aspires
Beyond thus high, insatiate to pursue
Vain war with Heaven; and, by success untaught,
His proud imaginations thus displayed:--
"Powers and Dominions, Deities of Heaven!--
For, since no deep within her gulf can hold
Immortal vigour, though oppressed and fallen,
I give not Heaven for lost: from this descent
Celestial Virtues rising will appear
More glorious and more dread than from no fall,
And trust themselves to fear no second fate!--
Me though just right, and the fixed laws of Heaven,
Did first create your leader--next, free choice
With what besides in council or in fight
Hath been achieved of merit--yet this loss,

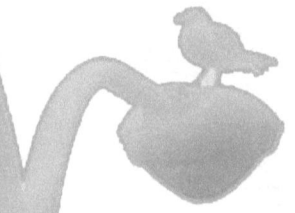

Dean Goodluck

Thus far at least recovered, hath much more
Established in a safe, unenvied throne,
Yielded with full consent. The happier state
In Heaven, which follows dignity, might draw
Envy from each inferior; but who here
Will envy whom the highest place exposes
Foremost to stand against the Thunderer's aim
Your bulwark, and condemns to greatest share
Of endless pain? Where there is, then, no good
For which to strive, no strife can grow up there
From faction: for none sure will claim in Hell
Precedence; none whose portion is so small
Of present pain that with ambitious mind
Will covet more! With this advantage, then,
To union, and firm faith, and firm accord,
More than can be in Heaven, we now return
To claim our just inheritance of old,
Surer to prosper than prosperity
Could have assured us; and by what best way,
Whether of open war or covert guile,
We now debate. Who can advise may speak."
He ceased; and next him Moloch, sceptred king,
Stood up--the strongest and the fiercest Spirit
That fought in Heaven, now fiercer by despair.

Six Steps Wiser - WcP Reading & Reflection Vol. 06

His trust was with th' Eternal to be deemed
Equal in strength, and rather than be less
Cared not to be at all; with that care lost
Went all his fear: of God, or Hell, or worse,
He recked not, and these words thereafter spake:--
"My sentence is for open war. Of wiles,
More unexpert, I boast not: them let those
Contrive who need, or when they need; not now.
For, while they sit contriving, shall the rest--
Millions that stand in arms, and longing wait
The signal to ascend--sit lingering here,
Heaven's fugitives, and for their dwelling-place
Accept this dark opprobrious den of shame,
The prison of his tyranny who reigns
By our delay? No! let us rather choose,
Armed with Hell-flames and fury, all at once
O'er Heaven's high towers to force resistless way,
Turning our tortures into horrid arms
Against the Torturer; when, to meet the noise
Of his almighty engine, he shall hear
Infernal thunder, and, for lightning, see
Black fire and horror shot with equal rage
Among his Angels, and his throne itself
Mixed with Tartarean sulphur and strange fire,

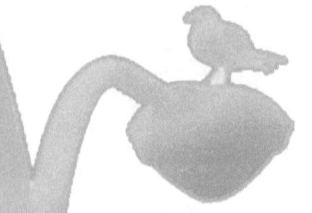

Dean Goodluck

His own invented torments. But perhaps
The way seems difficult, and steep to scale
With upright wing against a higher foe!
Let such bethink them, if the sleepy drench
Of that forgetful lake benumb not still,
That in our porper motion we ascend
Up to our native seat; descent and fall
To us is adverse. Who but felt of late,
When the fierce foe hung on our broken rear
Insulting, and pursued us through the Deep,
With what compulsion and laborious flight
We sunk thus low? Th' ascent is easy, then;
Th' event is feared! Should we again provoke
Our stronger, some worse way his wrath may find
To our destruction, if there be in Hell
Fear to be worse destroyed! What can be worse
Than to dwell here, driven out from bliss, condemned
In this abhorred deep to utter woe!
Where pain of unextinguishable fire
Must exercise us without hope of end
The vassals of his anger, when the scourge
Inexorably, and the torturing hour,
Calls us to penance? More destroyed than thus,
We should be quite abolished, and expire.

What fear we then? what doubt we to incense
His utmost ire? which, to the height enraged,
Will either quite consume us, and reduce
To nothing this essential--happier far
Than miserable to have eternal being!--
Or, if our substance be indeed divine,
And cannot cease to be, we are at worst
On this side nothing; and by proof we feel
Our power sufficient to disturb his Heaven,
And with perpetual inroads to alarm,
Though inaccessible, his fatal throne:
Which, if not victory, is yet revenge."
He ended frowning, and his look denounced
Desperate revenge, and battle dangerous
To less than gods. On th' other side up rose
Belial, in act more graceful and humane.
A fairer person lost not Heaven; he seemed
For dignity composed, and high exploit.
But all was false and hollow; though his tongue
Dropped manna, and could make the worse appear
The better reason, to perplex and dash
Maturest counsels: for his thoughts were low--
To vice industrious, but to nobler deeds
Timorous and slothful. Yet he pleased the ear,
And with persuasive accent thus began:--

Dean Goodluck

"I should be much for open war, O Peers,
As not behind in hate, if what was urged
Main reason to persuade immediate war
Did not dissuade me most, and seem to cast
Ominous conjecture on the whole success;
When he who most excels in fact of arms,
In what he counsels and in what excels
Mistrustful, grounds his courage on despair
And utter dissolution, as the scope
Of all his aim, after some dire revenge.
First, what revenge? The towers of Heaven are filled
With armed watch, that render all access
Impregnable: oft on the bodering Deep
Encamp their legions, or with obscure wing
Scout far and wide into the realm of Night,
Scorning surprise. Or, could we break our way
By force, and at our heels all Hell should rise
With blackest insurrection to confound
Heaven's purest light, yet our great Enemy,
All incorruptible, would on his throne
Sit unpolluted, and th' ethereal mould,
Incapable of stain, would soon expel
Her mischief, and purge off the baser fire,

Six Steps Wiser - WcP Reading & Reflection Vol. 06

Victorious. Thus repulsed, our final hope
Is flat despair: we must exasperate
Th' Almighty Victor to spend all his rage;
And that must end us; that must be our cure--
To be no more. Sad cure! for who would lose,
Though full of pain, this intellectual being,
Those thoughts that wander through eternity,
To perish rather, swallowed up and lost
In the wide womb of uncreated Night,
Devoid of sense and motion? And who knows,
Let this be good, whether our angry Foe
Can give it, or will ever? How he can
Is doubtful; that he never will is sure.

- from Paradise Lost: Book 02 (lines 1-154)
by John Milton

Dean Goodluck

A Gleam Of Sunshine

Six Steps Wiser - WcP Reading & Reflection Vol. 06

Poem
A Gleam Of Sunshine
Henry Wadsworth Longfellow

This is the place. Stand still, my steed,
Let me review the scene,
And summon from the shadowy Past
The forms that once have been.

The Past and Present here unite
Beneath Time's flowing tide,
Like footprints hidden by a brook,
But seen on either side.

Here runs the highway to the town;
There the green lane descends,
Through which I walked to church with thee,
O gentlest of my friends!

The shadow of the linden-trees
Lay moving on the grass;
Between them and the moving boughs,
A shadow, thou didst pass.

Thy dress was like the lilies,
And thy heart as pure as they:
One of God's holy messengers
Did walk with me that day.

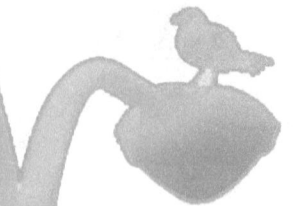

Dean Goodluck

I saw the branches of the trees
Bend down thy touch to meet,
The clover-blossoms in the grass
Rise up to kiss thy feet,

"Sleep, sleep to-day, tormenting cares,
Of earth and folly born!"
Solemnly sang the village choir
On that sweet Sabbath morn.

Through the closed blinds the golden sun
Poured in a dusty beam,
Like the celestial ladder seen
By Jacob in his dream.

And ever and anon, the wind,
Sweet-scented with the hay,
Turned o'er the hymn-book's fluttering leaves
That on the window lay.

Long was the good man's sermon,
Yet it seemed not so to me;
For he spake of Ruth the beautiful,
And still I thought of thee.

Long was the prayer he uttered,
Yet it seemed not so to me;
For in my heart I prayed with him,
And still I thought of thee.

But now, alas! the place seems changed;
Thou art no longer here:
Part of the sunshine of the scene
With thee did disappear.

Though thoughts, deep-rooted in my heart,
Like pine-trees dark and high,
Subdue the light of noon, and breathe
A low and ceaseless sigh;

This memory brightens o'er the past,
As when the sun, concealed
Behind some cloud that near us hangs
Shines on a distant field.

- A Gleam Of Sunshine
by Henry Wadsworth Longfellow

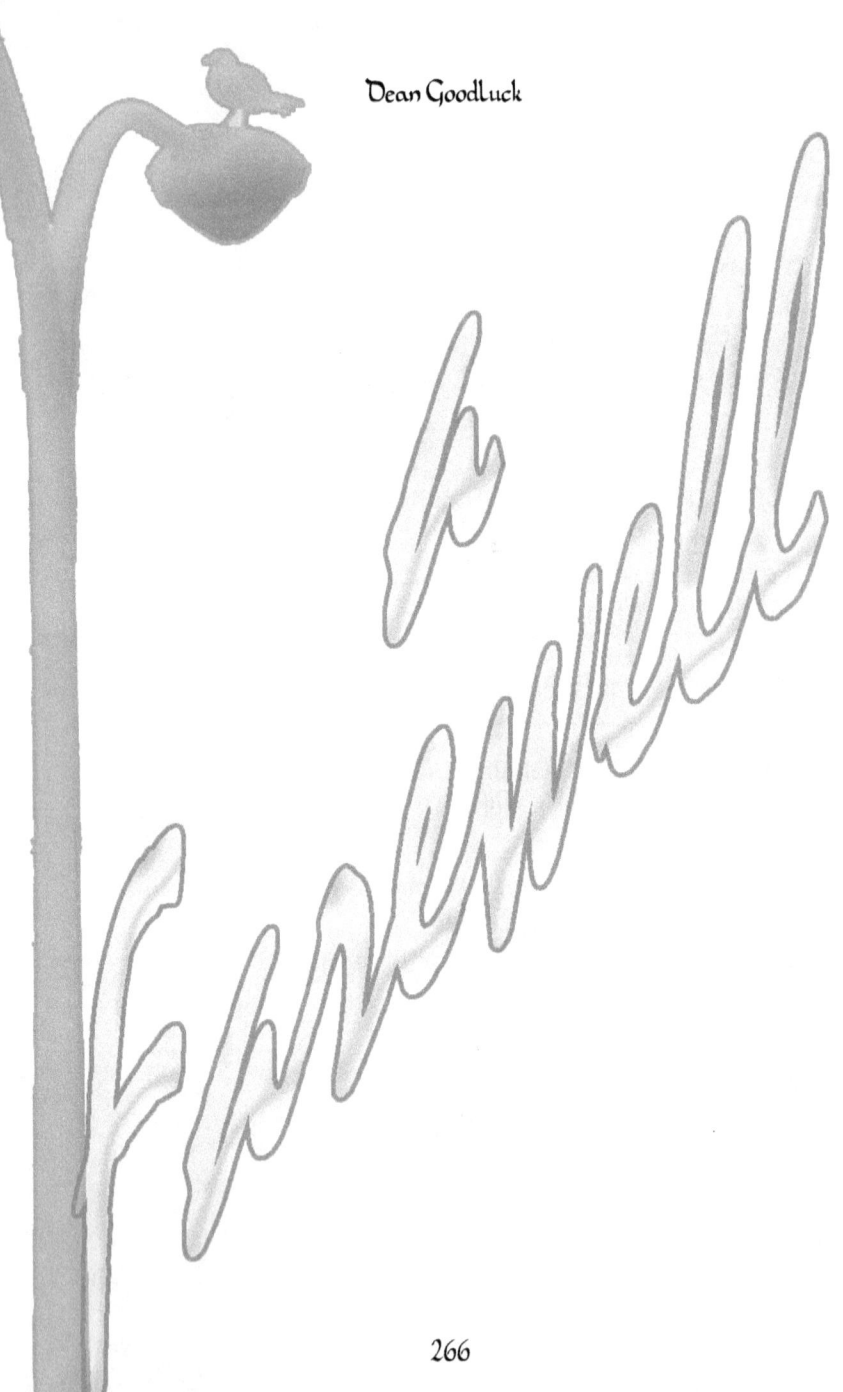

Dean Goodluck

A Farewell

Six Steps Wiser - WcP Reading & Reflection Vol. 06

Poem
A Farewell
– Alfred Lord Tennyson

Flow down, cold rivulet, to the sea,
Thy tribute wave deliver:
No more by thee my steps shall be,
For ever and for ever.

Flow, softly flow, by lawn and lea,
A rivulet then a river:
Nowhere by thee my steps shall be
For ever and for ever.

But here will sigh thine alder tree
And here thine aspen shiver;
And here by thee will hum the bee,
For ever and for ever.

A thousand suns will stream on thee,
A thousand moons will quiver;
But not by thee my steps shall be,
For ever and for ever.

- A Farewell
by Alfred Lord Tennyson

Publisher's Blog:
WcP Blog | World Culture Pictorial
www.worldculturepictorial.com

"I am just happy to know about your website.
It's informative and valuable for me.
Thanks for sharing interesting info with us.
Keep doing best in future."
- Kelvin

"Yes i agree with the above poem
that window is the world so far
i have come across. Every thing comes from it.
You have written in a very poetic way.
Looking forward for more poems from this."
- Anonymous

"I was so impressed by it I felt I would
reach out to you to say thank you.
Great work...
that's one great blog you've got there!"
- Kayla

Dean Goodluck

Other Volumes in the Series

full color print
through and through
including art images

www.worldculturepictorial.com/one-step-wiser.html

Six Steps Wiser - WcP Reading & Reflection Vol. 06

Other Volumes in the Series

full color print
through and through
including art images

www.worldculturepictorial.com/one-step-wiser.html

Dean Goodluck

Other Volumes in the Series

b&w interior print
on classic creme paper
including art images

www.worldculturepictorial.com/one-step-wiser.html

Six Steps Wiser - WcP Reading & Reflection Vol. 06